Praise for

Gay Marriage

"Rauch employs a smart and well-timed strategy. . . . This is a book that succeeds on its intellectual merits."
—*Los Angeles Times Book Review*

"From now on, any legitimate debate about gay marriage will have to take account of the case Rauch makes here."
—*Austin American-Statesman*

"[A] spirited defense of love and commitment . . . It's difficult to imagine a more useful book for explaining this controversial issue."
—*The Tennessean* (Nashville)

"This is a provocative book that's bound to cause a ruckus. . . . [Rauch makes] compelling, thoughtful points aimed right at the heart of conservative America."   —*The Globe and Mail* (Toronto)

"Working to convince rather than condemn, Rauch displays the rarest of qualities: empathy."   —*The News & Observer* (Raleigh)

"Throughout this deft and nimble work, Rauch . . . is unafraid to explore taboo issues . . . [with a] breezy, detailed, yet uncluttered style."   —*Washington Blade*

"Rauch has produced a political turning point. . . . With disciplined logic and unfailing humility, Rauch refutes the standard arguments against gay marriage. . . . There is hope for the future if even a few respond to Rauch's eloquent plea."
—*The Courier-Journal* (Louisville)

"This is a timely and readable book that will provoke people on both sides of the argument." —*Library Journal*

"Talk about perfect timing—perfect for a country that can no longer avoid resolving the controversy this book addresses. The argument about whether legal recognition of same-sex marriages is sound social policy has come to a rolling boil. And now one of Washington's most respected writers offers an exquisitely measured argument for the affirmative. Jonathan Rauch, a gay man in a long-term relationship, understands the lives as well as the laws at issue." —George F. Will

"By the time Jonathan Rauch finished writing this book, two fewer taboos were left standing. The first is the one against bringing reason to bear in the discussion of emotional political topics. And by violating taboo number one, he makes clear how little rational support there is for taboo number two—the case against allowing two people of the same sex to formalize their love through marriage. Rauch's articulation of the logical case for allowing same-sex couples to marry illustrates why so many of its opponents have decided to abandon logic in making their arguments." —Barney Frank

"Jonathan Rauch's reasoned and passionate brief for gay marriage, his wholehearted embrace of the obligations and traditions of marriage itself, and his compelling cautions against civil union alternatives to marriage will stand as a defining argument in the upcoming struggle over same-sex marriage. Agree or disagree, you have to read this book!" —Barbara Dafoe Whitehead

Gay Marriage

Gay Marriage

Why It Is Good for Gays, Good for Straights,

and Good for America

Jonathan Rauch

An Owl Book

Henry Holt and Company

New York

Henry Holt and Company, LLC
Publishers since 1866
115 West 18th Street
New York, New York 10011

Library of Congress Cataloging-in-Publication Data
Rauch, Jonathan, 1960–
  Gay marriage : why it is good for gays, good for straights, and good for
America / Jonathan Rauch.—1st ed.
     p.   cm.
  Includes index.
  ISBN-13: 978-0-8050-7815-2
  ISBN-10: 0-8050-7815-0
  1. Same-sex marriage—United States. 2. Civil rights—United States.
3. United States—Social life and customs. 4. United States—Politics
and government—2001– 5. United States—Social policy—1993– I. Title.

HQ1034.U5438   2004
306.84'8—dc22   2003068554

First published in hardcover in 2004 by Times Books
First Owl Books Edition 2005

Designed by Fritz Metsch

Printed in the United States of America

1   3   5   7   9   10   8   6   4   2

For Michael

Marry me, when we can

Contents

Introduction:
The Imagination Gap

Try to imagine life without marriage. If today you are married, imagine that tomorrow, as though in a Kafka tale, you wake up to find that your marriage has never occurred. Moreover, your marriage *cannot* occur. There is no one for you to marry, or at least no way for you to marry the person you love. Your spouse may still be with you but now is not your spouse at all, but your "partner," or your girlfriend or boyfriend or companion or live-in lover or significant other or just, so to speak, your squeeze. You are not exactly sure how to introduce this person. You and your companion may think of yourselves as married, but your friends and family and coworkers may not see you and your partner (or is it companion? or lover? or friend?) as married, and certainly the government and the law do not. Then again, perhaps you are single. Without the special bonds of marriage, and without the familial and social and legal support which marriage conveys, your relationship broke up during a bad patch a few years back. Now you are unattached, possibly looking for someone—someone whom you know you cannot marry. You are no longer a single person looking to marry or between marriages. You are between "relationships." That is not the same thing. Your future has changed, probably not for the better.

Now push your imagination a step further. Erase marriage not just from your present but from your past. Imagine looking back on a childhood and youth without the prospect of marriage. From the dawn of adolescence, when you first felt the beat of love in your breast, you have known that you would never marry anyone you felt passion for. Your first kiss was a kiss without hope of marriage. Your first date was a date without hope of marriage. When you discovered sex, it, too, was without hope of marriage. True love means, first and foremost, a love which ends in lasting marriage. For you, true love in that sense is not possible, and never has been possible, and you have grown up assuming it would never be possible. Your heart, now, is not the same heart. It has changed, and perhaps not for the better.

And now, if I may try your patience, push your imagination still further, to the outer limits of strangeness. Imagine not only yourself without marriage: imagine a whole community, a whole culture, without marriage. In your community, no one is married, no one has ever been married, no one ever will be married, and everyone has grown up from childhood taking the absence of marriage for granted. What is this community, your world, like? More unstable than the one you were accustomed to before your Kafkaesque metamorphosis, no doubt: probably less healthy, less happy; perhaps full of sex but not as full of love. It is a world of fragile families, a world marked by heightened fear of loneliness or abandonment in old age, a world in some respects not civilized, because marriage is the foundation of civilization.

Over time, many people in your marriageless world, possibly with you among them, succeed in forming and sustaining enduring attachments, and that success, against considerable odds, is a credit to human resilience. But, without society's help and encouragement, finding and forming lasting bonds has been hard. Even if, over time, most people in your marriageless world manage to pair off and act married, without marriage their relationships and their world are not the same. The law sees only individuals, never couples; the larger society is not sure what to make of these so-called partners. Their world remains incomplete, unfinished.

I think it is difficult, probably impossible, for most heterosexuals to imagine life without marriage. If, on the other hand, you are gay, you have not had to exercise your imagination much at all. For generations, homosexuals have come of age understanding that their love separated them from marriage instead of connecting them to it. They lived in a world turned upside down. As hard as it is now for heterosexuals to imagine life without marriage, that is how hard it was, until comparatively recently, for homosexuals to imagine life *with* marriage. If homosexuality has long seemed grotesque and threatening to heterosexuals, and if heterosexual convention has often seemed cruel and oppressive to homosexuals, the main reason is not the difference in sexual orientation as such but, rather, the marriage gap, which is really an imagination gap. Neither side could imagine the other's world. To be homosexual meant not to be married. To be married—happily and honestly married—meant not to be homosexual.

One of my childhood memories is of a day when, as I sat on the piano bench in the family room, it dawned on me that I would never be married. I have a distinct recollection of that moment. I did not discover or learn that I would never be married; I merely recognized that I knew it. That day was a long time, I think about fifteen years, before I understood I was homosexual. Throughout my childhood and youth, I had no notion of sexuality, but I did understand that marriage was not for me. Much later, after struggle and delay, I established caring relationships, but by that time I had grown up seeing life through the weird prism of marriagelessness. I assumed things would never change. I would never have two wings and fly, and I would never be married.

———

During the last decade of the twentieth century, a miracle happened, although some would call it a nightmare. In the early 1990s, gay people started talking as never before about getting married, and a lawsuit in Hawaii, where a same-sex couple sought a marriage license, forced the country to listen. The lawsuit failed (Hawaii foreclosed it by amending the state constitution), and the initial public reaction ranged from panicky to dismissive. Most states passed laws against same-sex marriage, and so did Congress. Some Americans kept listening, however. Polls showed that young people were not nearly so opposed to same-sex marriage as were their elders. A sprinkling of churches began to conduct gay wedding ceremonies (not legally binding, of course). The law edged toward same-sex marriage, too. Vermont's Supreme Court ordered legal parity for gay and straight unions, and the state responded with "civil unions" for homosexual couples. Some European countries moved in the same direction, with the Netherlands adopting full-blown gay marriage in 2001. The idea of gay marriage, though still politically hopeless, began to seem at least less bizarre.

Then, in 2003, something else happened. It was as if a trigger had been pulled and a gunshot was fired in a quiet room. A Canadian court ordered the province of Ontario to recognize same-sex marriages. Only days later, the United States Supreme Court struck down sodomy laws, in a decision—*Lawrence v. Texas*—which conservatives widely (and wrongly) believed would soon lead to the legalization of gay marriage by the federal courts. Gay activists used the sodomy decision as grounds to file suit in Arizona demanding a marriage license. (They lost.) Other Americans sued for U.S. recognition of Canadian gay marriages. Conservatives panicked. Some of them said not just that same-sex marriage might happen but that it was practically a done deal. Gay marriage, wrote Ramesh Ponnuru in *National Review*, was "not quite inevitable." In the same magazine's online edition, Maggie Gallagher, a conservative columnist, gave notice of the apocalypse. "We are poised to lose the gay-marriage battle badly," she said. "It means losing the marriage debate. It means losing limited government. It means losing American civilization." As if in answer, in November the Massachusetts Supreme Judicial Court declared the exclusion of gay couples from marriage to be in violation of the state's constitution, and ordered gay marriage starting in six months. "The marriage ban works a deep and scarring hardship on a very real segment of the community for no rational reason," ruled the court. "We construe civil marriage to mean the voluntary union of two persons as spouses, to the exclusion of all others." Even for friends of same-sex marriage, things seemed to be moving disconcertingly fast.

Massachusetts began issuing fully legal marriage licenses to gay couples. It was the beginning of what promised to be a political and social conflict of years' duration. Suddenly, and sooner than almost anyone had expected, the imagination gap snapped shut. Hardly anyone had been ready to imagine same-sex marriage. Now everyone must imagine it.

What might gay marriage do? That depends on the answer to another question, one which has received remarkably little systematic thought: What is marriage for? This book is an effort to answer both questions.

Same-sex marriage would be good for homosexuals. So I believe and so I will argue here. This book, however, is devoted to a larger proposition: that same-sex marriage is win-win-win. It is good for homosexuals, good for heterosexuals, and good for the institution of marriage: good, in other words, for American society. Far from opening the door to all sorts of scary redefinitions of marriage, from polygamy to incest to who knows what, same-sex marriage is the surest way to shut that door. Far from decoupling marriage from its core mission, same-sex marriage clarifies and strengthens that mission. Far from hastening the social decline of marriage, same-sex marriage shores up the key values and commitments on which couples and families and society depend. Far from dividing America and weakening communities, same-sex marriage, if properly implemented, can make the country both better unified and truer to its ideals.

No doubt, same-sex marriage would tend to normalize homosexuality—for homosexuals. (Not many straight people will be marrying someone of the same sex.) That, to my mind, would be a very good thing, because homosexuality *is* normal—for homosexuals. The main and great benefit of same-sex marriage, however, would be its normalization of marriage. Marriage depends for its success on its uniqueness and its universality. Those, in turn, depend on two principles. One is "If you want the benefits of marriage, you have to get married." The other is "Marriage is for everyone—no exclusions, no exceptions." Gay marriage reinforces both principles. It makes marriage not just *a* norm (the one for heterosexuals) but *the* norm (for everybody). In doing so, it offers the best hope of stopping the proliferation—aided, perversely, by the anti-gay-marriage movement—of marriage-like and "marriage-lite" alternatives.

Like change of any sort, same-sex marriage would entail costs as well as benefits. It would do harm as well as good. The trick, here as always, is to maximize the good and minimize the harm. That is why this book is devoted to a second proposition: there is a right way and a wrong way to move to same-sex marriage. The right way is gradually, one state at a time. Same-sex marriage will work best when people accept and understand it, whereas a sudden national enactment, if somehow it were to happen, might spark a culture war on the order of the abortion battle. Activists of the left and of the right join forces in insisting on an all-or-nothing approach (although one side wants all and the other wants nothing), but a middle way will be better by far. The United States is blessed with a federalist system which allows the states to experiment independently and learn from success and failure. Thus the

United States, probably alone among the countries of the developed world, is positioned to get gay marriage right.

————

As I hope you have gathered, I come to this as a true believer in the special importance and unique qualities of the institution of marriage. For all its failings in particular cases, and for all the stress it has borne lately, marriage is *the* great civilizing institution. No other institution has the power to turn narcissism into partnership, lust into devotion, strangers into kin. What other force can bond across clans and countries and continents and even cultures? In *Romeo and Juliet,* it was not the youths' love which their warring and insular clans feared; it was their marriage.

Unlike some people, therefore, I wouldn't support same-sex marriage as a matter of equal rights if I thought it would wreck opposite-sex marriage. Same-sex marriage is a big change. Advocates of gay marriage are trying to change the way things have been for—well, forever. I accept that the burden of proof is on my shoulders. My promise to you is to make my case as rigorously as I can, to resist cutting corners, and to confront the arguments against gay marriage in their strongest form. If you catch me in a cheap shot, I apologize. I further promise to challenge the opponents' arguments rather than their motives. The philosopher Sidney Hook once said: "*Before* impugning an opponent's motives, even when they may rightly be impugned, answer his arguments." That is the spirit in which this book is written. Some gay-marriage opponents may be bigoted or homophobic or otherwise out to get gay people, but most of them are motivated by a sincere desire to do what's best for their marriages, their children, their society. One thing above all, then, I promise to remember: this is *marriage* we're talking about. We must act carefully. We must think carefully.

————

This book is primarily for two kinds of people. If you are gay, it tries to show how marriage can change us—you and me, but especially the gay generations coming after ours—for the better. I'm well aware that not all gay people share my view of marriage and of the central part it plays in the good life. Although at times my enthusiasm may seem to suggest otherwise, in no way do I believe that marriage should be mandatory or that single people should be scorned or disrespected. My view, rather, is that marriage will give us the opportunity to become better people, by bestowing upon us the full responsibilities of adulthood.

If, on the other hand, you are not gay but are willing to approach marriage with a moderately open mind and some sympathy for gay people, this book tries to show that same-sex marriage is not only fair but also wise, not merely compared with its real-world alternatives but in its own right. I certainly don't expect you to agree with all that I say. In fact, I expect and hope you will push back. Whether or not same-sex marriage is actually enacted, it has already sparked a more serious and more thoughtful discussion of what marriage is all about than America has seen in many years. I will be happy merely to contribute something worthwhile to the discussion. This is not a book about gay marriage; it could not be just that and hope to succeed. This is a book about marriage.

Finally, a word to my nonaudience. Some readers will be anti-gay activists looking for ammunition against same-sex marriage. Fair enough, up to a point, and inevitable. Some people believe that homosexuality is wrong, period; some believe that real homosexuals (persons for whom opposite-sex love and marriage simply aren't options) don't actually exist; and some are, for whatever reason, beyond persuading that marriage can ever be anything other than the union of male and female. I can't expect to reach such readers. I can, however, make one request of them, which is to remember this: *standing still is not an option.* There is no going back to 1950. Homosexuals are increasingly open and ordinary and will not retreat into the closet. The days when homosexual unions—marital or nonmarital—were invisible are gone, and gone for good. Homosexual relationships will enjoy increasing social recognition and respect even outside marriage. If your first choice is for the whole gay thing to go away, remember that children can demand their first choice or nothing, but adults must often deal in second choices. If you can never accept same-sex marriage as just or moral, I ask you nonetheless to consider: If gay marriage is outlawed, what will come in its place? The world is changing, and marriage, like it or not, is changing, too.

1

What Is Marriage For?

When I was six years old, I went with my family from Phoenix, where I was born and raised, to visit New York. I remember only a little about that trip, apart from a visit to the Statue of Liberty, but seeing *Fiddler on the Roof* on Broadway remains vivid. It was my first play and a great play to boot, and Tevye's dream frightened me half to death, but another, more tender scene also stayed with me.

Tevye is a poor milkman in a Jewish shtetl (village) in czarist Russia. Life there is hardscrabble and traditional, and he is at first scandalized and then grudgingly helpful when his children break with custom by rejecting arranged marriages and insisting on marrying for love. Shaken, Tevye one day asks his wife, Golde: "Do you love me?"

The question strikes Golde as bizarre. "Do I *what*?" she sings. "Go inside, go lie down. Maybe it's indigestion." Tevye is undeterred and presses the question. "You're a fool!" his wife replies.

"But do you love me?"

"After twenty-five years," she grumbles, "why talk about love right now?" Still he insists: "Do you love me?"

"I'm your wife."

For Golde this is the answer. Or as much of an answer as she needs. She has done her job as a spouse; why would he want more? But Tevye sings on: "But do you love me?"

"Do I love him?"

And now, at last, she gives her answer:

For twenty-five years I've lived with him,
Fought with him, starved with him,
Twenty-five years my bed is his.
If that's not love, what is?

"Then you love me!" says Tevye.

"I suppose I do."

"And I suppose I love you, too."

The 1960s were the dawn of the era of love. Love was in the air, love was all around, all we needed was love, what the world needed now was love sweet love, love would keep us together, we should make love not war, we emblazoned LOVE on postage stamps and honored it with statues in public squares. Probably not coincidentally, it was also the age when the American divorce rate soared, to levels never before seen. Love was up, marriage was down. If the light of love dimmed in your marriage, or if it shined in new directions, then follow your heart. You and your partner and your children and everyone would be happier.

That was the air I breathed as I grew up, and yet even a six-year-old was capable of recognizing, in *Do You Love Me?*, a different and in some respects wiser view of love. Later on in my life, some years after my parents divorced (when I was twelve), it occurred to me to wonder: Did Tevye and Golde know something that many of us might have forgotten?

———

What is marriage for? That ought to be the easiest question in the world to answer. So many people get married, so much cultural experience has accumulated, and so many novels and dramas and counselors and manuals and "Dear Abby" columns crowd the world. Yet, until recently, when the gay-marriage debate forced the issue, hardly anyone gave much thought to the question. Such answers as were given were shallow or incoherent, especially at first. Gay activists said: Marriage is for love and we love each other, therefore we should be able to marry. Traditionalists said: Marriage is for procreation, and homosexuals do not procreate, therefore you should not be able to marry. That pretty well covered the spectrum. Secular thinking on the matter has been shockingly sketchy.

In its religious dress, marriage has a straightforward justification. It is as it is because that is how God wants it. As the Vatican said in 2003, "Marriage is not just any relationship between human beings. It was established by the Creator with its own nature, essential properties and purpose." Depending on the religion, God has various things to say about the nature and purpose of marriage. Modern marriage is, of course, based on traditions which religion helped to codify and enforce. But religious doctrine has no special standing in the world of secular law and policy, although it certainly holds and deserves influence. Moreover, a lot of what various religions say about marriage is inconsistent with or downright opposed to the consensus view of marriage today. The biblical patriarchs were polygamous and effectively owned their wives; in any number of religious traditions today, equality within marriage remains anathema. The law allows routine divorce and remarriage, something Jesus unequivocally condemned. If we want to know what marriage is for in modern America, we need a sensible secular doctrine.

You could try the dictionary. If you did, you might find something like: "**marriage** (n). The formal union of a man and woman, typically recognized by law, by which they become husband and wife" (*Oxford American College Dictionary*). Not much help there. Or: "**marriage** (n). The state of being married; a legal contract, entered into by a man and a woman, to live together as husband and wife" (*Funk & Wagnalls Standard College Dictionary*). Maybe your dictionary does better.

You could turn to the statute books. Law is, after all, dense with legal prerogatives enjoyed by married couples and dense with cases (often divorces) allocating assets and resolving conflicts. But you will find surprisingly little about what marriage is for and what must or must not, or should or should not, go on within it. Instead, you will find definitions like the one a Washington State court provided in a 1974 case in which two men tried to get a marriage license. Marriage, said the court, is defined as "the legal union of one man and one woman." The case revealed marriage, writes the philosopher Richard Mohr, "at least as legally understood, to be nothing but an empty space, delimited only by what it excludes—gay couples."

One way to get a handle on what marriage is for would be to ask what married people must do. Or, at a bare minimum, what it is they must *not* do in order to remain married. Here, astonishingly, the answer turns out to be, more or less: nothing. Nearly all civic institutions require you to do or not do at least something. If you want to be a voter, you need to register, re-register when you move, go to the polls, prove your identity, and vote in a specified manner. In many places, if you are convicted of a felony, you lose your vote. If you want to own property, you have to buy it legally (often a complicated process) and pay applicable taxes, or it will cease to be yours. If you want to be a driver, you must prove you can drive safely and see adequately; if you disobey the rules or lose your sight, your license may be revoked. By contrast, few if any behaviors automatically end a marriage. If a man beats his wife—about the worst thing he can do to her—he may be convicted of assault, but the marriage is not automatically dissolved. Couples can be adulterous (or "open") yet still be married, as long as that is what they choose to be. They can be celibate, too; consummation is not required. They can live together or apart, in the same house or in different countries: there is no residency or cohabitation requirement. There is no upper age limit. Spouses need not know each other or even meet before receiving a marriage license. They need not regularly see each other; a prisoner of war or a sailor or an adventurer can be separated from his wife for years and be no less married. They can have children or not. Not only can felons marry, they can do so on their way to the electric chair.

Secular law nowadays makes all sorts of provisions for people who *are* married, but it sets only a few rules for people who want to *get* married. Marriage happens only with the consent of the parties. The parties are not children. The number of parties is two. The parties are not closely related. One is a man and the other is a woman.

Within those rules, a marriage is whatever the spouses agree it is. So the laws say almost nothing about what marriage is for: just who can be married. All in all, it is an impressive and also rather astonishing victory for modern individualism that so important an institution should be bereft of any formal social instruction as to what should go on inside it.

————

What is marriage for? If the dictionaries and the law are of little help, perhaps we can find clues by asking: What *was* marriage for? A backward glance, however, sheds less light than one might hope. Mostly what it establishes is that, in the past century and more, marriage has changed nearly beyond recognition.

Most cultures, throughout history, have been polygamous. One man marries several women, at least in society's upper echelons. (The converse, one woman marrying several men, is rare, almost unheard of.) Polygamy was largely about hierarchy: it helped men to dominate women, and it helped high-status men, with their multiplicity of highly desirable wives, dominate low-status men. The higher a man's status, the more wives he typically had. Among human societies, as among animals, it is monogamy that is the rarity. "A huge majority—980 of the 1,154 past or present societies for which anthropologists have data—have permitted a man to have more than one wife," says Robert Wright in *The Moral Animal: The New Science of Evolutionary Psychology* (1994). "And that number includes most of the world's hunter-gatherer societies, societies that are the closest thing we have to a living example of the context of human evolution."

The imposition of monogamy was an important step toward the development of modern liberalism, a point I will come back to in chapter 7. The advent of monogamy did not, however, make for anything like modern marriage. For, in secular society, marriage was largely a matter of business: cementing family ties, forging social or economic alliances, providing social status for men and economic security for women, conferring dowries, and so on. Marriages were typically arranged, and "love" in the modern sense was certainly no prerequisite. Family, in the days before the modern corporation, was business, and marriages were mergers and acquisitions. It would have seemed silly, under the circumstances, to allow individuals to marry on the basis of anything as whimsical as infatuation, or at least to allow marriages that were not carefully vetted and specifically approved by family elders. Elopement, in the upper social strata, was not only a scandal but a blow to a family's stability and standing. E. J. Graff, in her book *What Is Marriage For?* (1999), quotes from an eighteenth-century advice manual: "Children are so much the goods, the possessions of their parents, that they cannot, without a kind of theft, give themselves away without the allowance of those that have the right in them." Anyone who has read Jane Austen knows that the economic and business aspects of marriage remained prominent well into the nineteenth century.

In the recent past, and in some predominantly religious quarters to this day, marriage was about gender specialization. Men rightly do certain things, and women rightly do others, and to form a complete social unit, the two sexes must form a complementary partnership. Marriage is that partnership. Here again, love may be desirable, but it is no prerequisite. A marriage is successful if the two partners are conscientiously fulfilling their roles: the man attending to work and the world of affairs, the woman to home and children. In Japan today, remnants of this system persist, and it works surprisingly well. Spouses view their marriage as a partnership: an investment in security and status for themselves and their children. Because Japanese couples don't expect as much emotional fulfillment as Americans do, they are less inclined to break up. They also take a somewhat more relaxed attitude toward adultery. As long as each partner is doing his or her job, what's a little extracurricular activity?

In contemporary America, women expect to have opportunities to work outside the home, and men are expected to change diapers and even, however ineptly, help with the dishes. Marriage-as-business and marriage-as-gender-specialization linger only as vestiges. In the West today, of course, love is a defining element. Love sustains marriage, many people will tell you, and marriage sanctifies love—but it is the love, not the marriage, which makes the bond. That was the view I grew up with.

The notion of lifelong love is charming, if ambitious, and certainly love is a desirable and important element of marriage. In the modern world, a loveless wedding is not likely to produce a lasting marriage. Love is not, however, the defining element of marriage in society's eyes, and it never has been. You may or may not love your husband, but the two of you are just as married either way. You may love your mistress, but that does not make her your wife. To a large extent, marriage is defined not in tandem with love but in contradistinction to it: marriage is special precisely because it imposes obligations whether or not you and your spouse love each other. Love helps make sense of marriage from an emotional point of view, but it is not particularly important in making sense of marriage from the social-policy point of view.

With the rise of the gay-marriage debate, another view has come to the fore: marriage is about children. Rather than take this up here, I'll reserve it for chapter 6. At present, suffice to say that marriage is unquestionably good for children, but children are not and cannot be the only reason for marriage. No society denies marriage to the infertile; no society requires couples to promise they will have children; no society nullifies marriage if children don't turn up; for that matter, no modern society mandates marriage if they do. For the record, I would be the last to deny that children are a central reason for the privileged status of marriage. When men and women get together, children are a likely outcome; and, as we are learning in all sorts of unpleasant ways, when children appear without two parents, many kinds of trouble can follow. Without belaboring the point, I hope I won't be accused of saying that children are a trivial reason for marriage. They just cannot be the only reason.

What are the others? I can think of several possibilities, such as the provision of economic security for women (or men), or the orderly transfer of cultural and financial capital between families or generations. There is a lot of intellectual work to be done to sort the essential from the inessential purposes of marriage. It seems to me, however, that the two strongest candidates are these: settling the young, particularly young men; and providing reliable care-givers. Both purposes are critical to the functioning of a humane, stable society, and both are better served by marriage—that is, by one-to-one lifelong commitment—than by any other institution.

————

We all need a home; humans are nesting animals. Odysseus bore his trials by keeping the memory of home alive. Countless generations of soldiers and wanderers have done the same. Home may be a place or it may be a nomadic community; it can mean parents, friends, familiar customs, native language, citizenship, and the pub or pool hall down the block. For many people, however, it means one thing above all. It is the place where someone waits for you.

Leaving aside children, young adults are the people who need home the most and who have it the least. For many people, the period we call "leaving home"—leaving one's parents' home—is a time of great excitement but also great vulnerability. Most of us, at age eighteen or twenty-two, aren't yet very good at managing life. We lack status and feel less beholden to the society around us than we will later on, when we have money or memberships or mortgages. We want a lot of sex but tend to have trouble handling it. And, often, we are lonely.

The result can be trouble: idleness, depression, debauchery, drugs, unwanted pregnancy, an unwanted child. The problems of young men are especially worrisome, for society as well as for the young men.

"Men are more aggressive than women," writes James Q. Wilson, the prominent political scientist, in his 1993 book *The Moral Sense*. "In every known society, men are more likely than women to play roughly, drive recklessly, fight physically, and assault ruthlessly, and these differences appear early in life." He goes on to speak of the male's need to hunt, defend, attack.

> Much of the history of civilization can be thought of as an effort to adapt these male dispositions to contemporary needs by restricting aggression or channeling it into appropriate channels. That adaptation has often required extraordinary measures, such as hunting rituals, rites of passage, athletic contests, military discipline, guild apprenticeships, or industrial authority.

Most of the men I know are gentle souls, hardly uncivilized. Remember, though, that men often change when they gather in groups—or packs, or gangs. Wherever unattached young men gather in packs, you see no end of mischief: wildings in Central Park, gangs in Los Angeles, football hooligans in Britain, skinheads in Germany, hazings in college fraternities, gang bangs in prisons, grope lines in the military, and, in a different but ultimately no less tragic way, the bathhouses and wanton sex of gay San Francisco or New York in the 1970s. It is probably fair to say that civilizing young men is one of any society's two or three biggest problems.

"Of all the institutions through which men may pass—schools, factories, the military—marriage has the largest effect," writes Wilson. The stabilizing and settling effect of marriage is unmatched. "An unmarried man between twenty-four and thirty-five years of age is about three times as likely to murder another male as is a married man the same age," observes Wright. "He is also more likely to incur various risks—committing robbery, for example—to gain the resources that may attract women. He is more likely to rape."

Marriage confers status: to be married, in the eyes of society, is to be grown up. Marriage creates stakes: someone depends on you. Marriage creates a safe harbor for sex. Marriage puts two heads together, pooling experience and braking impulsiveness. Of all the things a young person can do to move beyond the vulnerabilities of early adulthood, marriage is far and away the most fruitful. We all need domesticating, not in the veterinary sense but in a more literal, human sense: we need a home. We are different people when we have a home: more stable, more productive, more mature, less self-obsessed, less impatient, less anxious. And marriage is the great domesticator.

Nowadays, of course, people marry later. A lot of people don't marry until their thirties. But civilization is not unraveling and packs of marauding youths have not taken over the streets. If marriage is so important to settling down, why do so many people manage to settle down *before* marrying?

The answer, I think, is this: marriage is a great domesticator, but so is the *prospect* of marriage. If you hope to get married, and if your friends and peers hope to get married, you will socialize and date more carefully. If you're a young woman, you will avoid getting pregnant unintentionally or gaining what used to be called a reputation. If you're a young man, you will reach for respectability. You will devote yourself to your work, try to build status, and earn money to make yourself marriageable (often true of women, too). People who expect to get married observe and emulate husbands and wives. For those on the path toward marriage, most of what they do is conditioned by the assumption that single life is a temporary phase. Because you aspire to marry, you prepare to marry. You make yourself what people used to call marriage material.

Nothing I've just said is intended to imply that people who don't want to get married or who don't manage to get married (a small minority, as it happens: about 90 percent of Americans get married) are uncivilized, dangerous, or pathetic. The point is that, whether you marry or not, it is the prospect and the possibility of marriage that makes us a society of homebodies, which is a wonderful thing to be.

————

Of course, women and older men do not generally travel in marauding or orgiastic packs. As the years go by, even the most impetuous tend to settle down. In that respect, age does some of the same work as marriage (and vice versa; ask any comedian). As life goes on, however, a second core rationale for marriage comes more strongly into play.

I have a good job. I have money. I have health insurance. I have friends. I have relatives. But my relatives live far away. My friends are busy. And no amount of money can allay what has to be one of the most elemental fears humans can know: the fear of enduring some catastrophe alone. Tomorrow, maybe, my little car gets hit by a big bus. Everything goes black. When I awake, I am surrounded by doctors and nurses, but without someone there especially for me, I am alone in the sense that matters most. I lose the power to work or walk or feed myself. A service comes by to check on me once a day. Meals on Wheels brings lunch. Nonetheless, I am alone. No one is there for *me*. God forbid it should ever happen. But we all know the fear.

Society worries, too. A second enormous problem for society is what to do when someone is beset by catastrophe. It could be cancer, a broken back, unemployment, depression; it could be exhaustion from work, stress under pressure, or an all-consuming rage. From society's point of view, an unattached person is an accident waiting to happen. The burdens of contingency are likely to fall, immediately and sometimes crushingly, on people— relatives, friends, neighbors—who have enough problems of their own, and then on charities and welfare agencies. We all suffer periods of illness, sadness, distress, fury. What happens to us, and what happens to the people around us, when we desperately need a hand but find none to hold?

If marriage has any meaning at all, it is that when you collapse from a stroke, there will be another person whose "job" is to drop everything and come to your aid. Or that when you come home after being fired, there will be someone to talk you out of committing a massacre or killing yourself. To be married is to know there is someone out there for whom you are always first in line.

No group could make such a commitment in quite the same way, because of a free-rider problem. If I were to marry three or four people, the pool of potential caregivers would be larger, but the situation would, perversely, make all of them less reliable: each could expect one of the others to take care of me (and each may be reluctant to do more than any of the others are willing to do—a common source of conflict among siblings who need to look after an aging parent). The pair bond, one to one, is the only kind which is inescapably reciprocal, perfectly mutual. Because neither of us has anyone else, we are there for each other.

All by itself, marriage is society's first and, often, second and third line of support for the troubled individual. A husband or wife is the social worker of first resort, the psychiatrist of first resort, the cop and counselor and insurer and nurse and 911 operator of first resort. Married people are happier, healthier, and live longer; married men have lower rates of homicide, suicide, accidents, and mental illness. In 1858, reports Graff, a British public-health statistician named William Farr noticed that, on average, married people outlive singles. "Marriage," said Farr, "is a healthy state. The single individual is much more likely to be wrecked on his voyage than the lives joined together in matrimony." Graff goes on to say:

> The data have been eerily consistent ever since: whether measuring by death rate, morbidity (health problems such as diabetes, kidney disease, or ischemic heart disease), subjective or stress-related complaints (dizziness, shortness of breath, achiness, days in bed during past year, asthma, headaches), or psychiatric problems (clinical depression or debilitating anxiety after a cancer diagnosis), married people do better than unmarried—single, widowed, divorced.

Might that just be because healthier people are more likely to marry? Maybe. But the conclusion remains the same even when studies compare matched populations, factor out confounding variables, or follow individuals over time. Moreover, married people do better than cohabiting couples, and their unions are more enduring—and, again, the generalization seems to hold even when researchers account for the fact that cohabitors and married people may be different. Marriage itself appears to be good for you. Why? I'm sure the answer is complicated. But in large part it must boil down to something pretty simple. Married people have someone to look after them, and they know it.

The gay-marriage debate is a storm that swirls around a single question. What makes marriage marriage? That is, what are marriage's essential attributes, and what are its incidental ones? As we will see, various people give various answers. They point to children, for instance. Or the ability to have children. Or heterosexual intercourse. Or monogamy. Clearly, marriage has many important attributes, and it would be unrealistic to expect agreement on what counts the most. But I think one attribute is more important than any of the others. If I had to pare marriage to its essential core, I would say that marriage is two people's lifelong commitment, recognized by law and by society, to care for each other. To get married is to put yourself in another person's hands, and to promise to take that person into your hands, and to do so within a community which expects both of you to keep your word.

Because, in theory, there is no reason why a male-male or female-female couple could not make and sustain the promise of lifelong caregiving, opponents of same-sex marriage are reluctant to put the caregiving commitment at the heart, rather than the periphery, of marriage. Against them, I adduce what I think are three strong kinds of evidence that caregiving is at the core of marriage: law, social opinion, and something else.

Law, as I said earlier, says almost nothing about what married people must do in order to be married; but it does weave a dense entanglement of prerogatives and special standings around any couple legally deemed to be wed. Spouses are generally exempted from having to testify against each other in court. They can make life-or-death decisions on each other's behalf in case of incapacity. They have hospital visitation rights. A doctor cannot refuse to tell them their spouse's condition. They have inheritance rights. They can file taxes as a single unit. On and on. The vast majority of the ways in which the law recognizes marriage—practically all of them, if you stop to think about it—aim at facilitating and bolstering the caregiving commitment. They are tools of trust and teamwork. A husband can speak to his wife candidly without fear that she will be served with a subpoena and rat him out. When one spouse is gravely ill, doctors and friends and other family members defer to the second spouse as caregiver in chief. Because spouses make a unique commitment to care for each other in life, their assets are presumed to merge when one of them dies—a recognition of what each has given up for the other. Most of what are usually thought of as the legal benefits of marriage are really gifts with strings attached. Or maybe strings with gifts attached. The law is saying: "You have a unique responsibility to care for each other. Here are the tools. Do your job."

Marriage creates kin. In olden times, marriage merged families to create alliances between clans. Today, marriage takes two people who are (except very rarely) not even remotely related and makes them each other's closest kin. Matrimony creates family out of thin air. Children cannot do this, nor can money, monogamy (that's just "going steady"), or lawyers. Only marriage does it.

Social opinion, I think, follows the same principle. Legally speaking, spouses are married until officially divorced. Socially speaking, however, under what circumstance would you regard someone as not just an imperfect spouse but as a nullifier of the marriage compact—a nonspouse? Adultery springs to mind. But the world is full of spouses who cheat or have cheated and who still manage to carry on in marriage. About 20 percent of American husbands admit to infidelity. Perhaps the betrayed spouse doesn't know, or knows but has forgiven, or has decided to live with the situation. I know more than one couple who have been through an adultery crisis and survived. An adulterous spouse is not a good spouse but, in the eyes of most people, would be a flawed spouse rather than a nonspouse.

What would lead me to think of someone as a nonspouse? Only, I think, abandonment. Mrs. Smith is diagnosed with a brain tumor. She will need treatment and care. Mr. Smith, an able-bodied adult with no history of mental illness, responds by leaving town. Now and then he calls her, chats for a few minutes as a friend might do, and then goes on about his business. He leaves Mrs. Smith in the hands of her sister, who has to fly in from Spokane. When the doctors call, he lets the answering machine take a message. "She can sign on our bank account," he says. "Let her hire help."

I have heard of people getting divorced in the face of a crisis. But I have never heard of anyone behaving like Mr. Smith while claiming to be married; and if Mr. Smith behaved that way, even his closest friends would think him beyond the pale. They would say he was having a breakdown—"not himself" (meaning, no longer the husband Mrs. Smith thought she had). Everyone else would just be shocked. Mrs. Smith, if she survived, would get a divorce.

Decent opinion has understood for centuries that, whatever else marriage may be, it is a commitment to be there. In 1547 (according to Graff), Archbishop Thomas Cranmer wrote that marriage is for "mutual society, help, and comfort, that the one ought to have of the other, both in prosperity and in adversity." I mentioned a third strong kind of evidence for my view that the prime-caregiver status is the sine qua non of marriage. Here it is:

> To have and to hold from this day forward, for better for worse, for richer for poorer, in sickness and in health, to love, cherish, and to obey, till death us do part.

I doubt there is a single grown-up person of sound mind in America who does not know what those words signify. They are from the Book of Common Prayer, dating from 1662. "Obey" is gone today, but otherwise not much has changed in four and a half centuries:

> Wilt thou love her, comfort her, honor and keep her in sickness and in health; and, forsaking all others, keep thee only unto her, so long as ye both shall live?

So go the ancient vows, the first for her, the second for him. The text speaks twice of care and comfort "in sickness and in health," twice of love, twice of a lifetime bond. Those three, it implies, are interwoven: the commitment to care for another for life is the love which exceeds all others, the love of another even above oneself. There is no promise of children here, either to have them or to raise them, no mention of sex, no mention of inheritance, not a word about personal fulfillment. Perhaps the writers of the vow meant to put in those things but forgot. Or perhaps they placed at the center of marriage what most married people today also place there: "in sickness and in health, to love and cherish, till death us do part."

———

I know a couple who have been married, now, for sixty years. I know them well, although it would not be proper to name them. But they are people I love.

Often it is hard to spend time with them, because they needle each other, raise their voices, speak harshly—not all the time, but often, and almost always unnecessarily. One says, "Where's your coat?" and the other says, "Whatsa matter, I always have to have a coat?" They do not show affection for each other. If this is love, it is not the kind of love I would prefer for myself. It's not the kind of marriage I would like, either.

The wife freely admits that the marriage has not been pleasant for many years. So I asked her: Why did you stick with it? Because, she said, for her generation divorce just wasn't something you thought about. Because, after a certain point, inertia took over. But then she said something else, something which, from the sudden firmness in her voice, I took to be her real answer. "Jon," she said, "he has been there for me. He has *always* been there. Whenever I needed him, he came through."

Tevye and Golde concluded that they must love each other, or else what could you call their twenty-five years of living and fighting and starving together? They were singing, of course, not about passionate love, or romantic love, or erotic love. They were singing of the unique kind of love which grows between two people who learn they can trust each other through anything. They were singing about marriage.

2

Accept No Substitutes

A few days before I began writing this chapter, I sat down to breakfast at a Washington hotel with a prominent conservative writer—a man who, like so many Americans, feels no animus toward homosexuals, indeed wishes them healthy and happy lives, but who is deeply reluctant to tamper with as venerable and important a tradition as marriage. Could we not, he wondered, have the best of both worlds? "Tell me," he said, "why wouldn't civil unions solve this problem?"

For some conservatives, there is no problem to solve. Homosexuals can't marry, and their relationships enjoy no social or legal support. Fine. Their relationships are wicked or trivial, and society has no interest in supporting them; if homosexuals are unhappy, their trouble is their homosexuality, not their marriage-lessness. They should become "ex-gays" by praying or getting therapy; or they should repress their sexual desires, pretend to be heterosexual, and fool straight people into marrying them; or they should just go away and stop rocking the boat.

Americans, to their credit, are less and less willing to take such dismissive positions. As more homosexuals come out into the open, more heterosexuals come to realize that homosexuality really exists: that is, there really are people for whom opposite-sex love is not an option, people who nonetheless need love and attachment as much as anybody else. What does society owe such people—and what, for that matter, do they owe society?

In the last few years, two quite different answers have emerged, both of them attempts to cope with gay people's marriagelessness without creating new problems for marriage. One answer might be called privatization, the other substitution—or, as I enjoy calling it, the ABM pact.

Privatizers are primarily libertarians, but they also include a sizable contingent of left-liberals. "Homosexuals have a valid complaint," they say. "It doesn't seem fair to exclude them from civil marriage. But why should there be civil marriage in the first place? Why should the government be in the business of deciding who can marry and who can't? Those judgments rightly belong to individuals. It's not the state's job to privilege one kind of family life over all the others. That is not only unfair, it's unnecessary. If we abolished civil marriage, there would still be lots of marriages. Religious people would marry in their faith and adhere to its marital dictates. Secular people would choose the terms of their own marriage and make a legal contract accordingly. (That sounds like a lot of paperwork, but most people would probably use one of a few standard forms. Anyway, why shouldn't people pay some attention to what they're getting into?) Instead of picking and choosing among relationships, the law would get out of the way. The result would be to make more people happy with their marriages, while sidestepping altogether the looming culture war over state recognition of same-sex unions."

Substituters are not eager to abolish civil marriage; to them, doing so would throw out the baby with the bathwater. "The state has an important role to play in defining and legitimizing marriage," they say. "And the state should steer clear of delegitimizing marriage by redefining it to include same-sex unions. But it is the symbolism of marriage which people are trying to preserve. They don't mind if gay people can put their partners on the company health plan, or if gay people get hospital visitation rights, or if they get inheritance rights. In fact, doing those things seems fair. And aren't such benefits what homosexuals really want and need anyway? Sure, they might prefer a piece of paper from the government, suitable for framing. But nowadays most couples probably can't even find their marriage license. The important thing for gay people is the substance, not the label. So set up 'domestic partnership' programs or 'civil unions' which confer many of the key benefits of marriage. Call the arrangements anything you like—just *don't call them marriage.*"

I call this the ABM pact, for Anything But Marriage. In effect, homosexuals and heterosexuals make a deal. Homosexuals get many of the benefits of marriage, and heterosexuals keep the official designation, with its symbolic and religious baggage. It seems a clever and humane compromise, and indeed it is rapidly becoming the consensus choice in the United States and Europe. Everybody wins, right?

Wrong.

Domestic-partner and other marriage-lite arrangements, as I can't resist calling them, do not give homosexuals what they need. They also do not give society what *it* needs. Although not necessarily calamitous, a multitrack system featuring marriage and various forms of pseudomarriage is, at best, a distant second choice to same-sex marriage—not just from homosexuals' point of view but from society's. As for the privatizing approach, it is probably the worst option of all.

The two approaches fail, at bottom, for the same reason: they misapprehend what marriage is. One sees marriage as a contract between two people. The other sees it as a package of benefits. Well, marriage is indeed both. But it is something much more.

———

In the preceding chapter, I sang the praises of marriage's near-magical ability to create kin out of thin air, to turn passion into commitment, to make people healthier and happier, and so forth. From my description, you might assume that I see marriage as some kind of sorcerer's wand: wave it over two people, and their love and lives are transformed.

Would it were so. In fact, as many people know all too well, the marriage vow is not a magical incantation. The weeks and months and then years after the wedding are sometimes harder than the weeks or months or years before. Marriages often fail, sometimes unavoidably. To understand how to preserve the health of marriage as a social institution, and also to understand why there is no substitute for same-sex marriage, it is necessary to understand where marriage gets its special power: how it works. And this depends crucially on understanding that marriage is not merely a contract between two people. It is a contract between two people *and their community.*

For most people, marrying, especially for the first time, is a very big decision. Not for everyone: some people exchange vows in Las Vegas as a lark. But for most, getting married is a life-changing event, one which demarcates the boundary between two major phases of life. Many men and women agonize about marrying. Am I ready? Is he or she the one? And many spouses remember their wedding day vividly for the rest of their lives. People may make many big decisions in life: to join the military, go to graduate school, buy a house, have children, donate a kidney. Yet probably no decision is quite as pregnant with meaning—with the sense of passing across a great divide—as is the decision to marry.

Why should marrying be such a big deal? Partly because the promise being made is extraordinary. That answer, however, begs the question. Why do people take this promise so seriously? The law has made it ever easier for two people to marry, no questions asked, no parental approval needed, no money down. Divorcing is easier, too. Under today's laws, young people could casually marry and divorce every six months as a way of shopping around; but they don't. Most people can expect that marriage will result in parenthood, and parenthood is certainly a momentous thing. Yet even people who, for whatever reason, do not want or cannot have children take marriage seriously. So the questions stand out in sharp relief. Why do we see marrying as one of life's epochal decisions? What gives the institution such mystique, such force?

I believe the answer is, in two words, *social expectations*.

When two people approach the altar or the bench to marry, they approach not only the presiding official but all of society. They enter into a compact not just with each other but with the world, and that compact says: "We, the two of us, pledge to make a home together, care for one another, and, perhaps, raise children together. In exchange for the caregiving commitment we are making, you, our community, will recognize us not only as individuals but as a bonded pair, a *family*, granting us a special autonomy and a special status which only marriage conveys. We, the couple, will support one another. You, society, will support us. You expect us to be there for each other and will help us meet those expectations. We will do our best, until death do us part."

In every marriage, social expectations are an invisible third partner. Friends, neighbors, parents, and in-laws heap blessings and congratulations on newlyweds, but their joy conveys an implicit injunction: "Be a good husband or wife. We're counting on you." Around the pair is woven a web of expectations that they will spend nights together, socialize together, make a home together—behavior which helps create a bond between them and make them feel responsible for each other. ("It's one A.M. Do you know where your spouse is?" Chances are you do.) Each spouse knows that he or she will get the first phone call when the other is in trouble or in need; and each knows that the expected response is to drop everything and deal with the problem.

Announce to your friends and coworkers that you're getting married, and they say not "That's interesting" or "Best of luck," but "That's wonderful! Congratulations!" Announce it to a parent, and frequently the reaction will be tearful. Stag parties and bridal showers signal that what is beginning is not just a new legal status or a new romantic episode or a new housing arrangement but rather a new stage of life. Expensive gifts deter casual commitment and make bailing out embarrassing. Many of the gifts are household items, appropriate for people about to make a home. The gifts express affection, but each comes with a hidden message: "We expect."

Then there is the wedding. It is not just a social occasion; it is a whole social technology. A few people (my sister, for one) hold private weddings with, at most, a handful of guests; but even the most private wedding involves not two people but three. Two people cannot marry each other; they must marry before a member of the clergy or a magistrate or clerk—someone to be the eyes and ears of society. In that sense, all weddings are public. If two people say their vows in the forest, with no one else around, they are not really married at all.

Most weddings, of course, are not just public ceremonies but major events. The most important people in the partners' lives—their families above all—are invited, and many of them come, sometimes traveling across the country or the world. The partners want to affirm their commitment not just in each other's eyes but in the eyes of the people who matter most. Each implicitly says to the other: "All of these people—my family, my friends, and your people, too—have heard my vow. That tells you I meant what I said." Often, though, it is the parents, especially the mothers, who want a really big wedding. The pride they express in their children's matrimony is another subtle—maybe not so subtle—way to say, "We have a stake in this union, too." A hundred witnesses, five hundred, they all heard the couple express their commitment. The presence of the guests, their joy, their smiles and snuffles, stamp the day as a rite of passage. The vows are sealed by the tears of the mothers in the front row: tears which tell the couple and the world, "This promise is important. This promise is like no other."

After the wedding come countless smaller gestures of community recognition and community interest. From now on, invitations arrive addressed to two people, not just one. Polite people do not neglect to say, "Give my best to your husband" or "How's the wife?"—casual reminders that, in the world's eyes, you're attached to somebody. If things go badly, expressions of concern and sometimes gossipy chitchat ("Why does she put up with that cheating bastard Frank?") quietly reinforce the community's stake. Anniversary parties bring together friends and family to celebrate that the marriage is intact (no awkward questions asked). The magic of marriage is that it wraps each partnership in a dense web of social expectations, and uses a hundred informal mechanisms to reinforce those expectations.

Law matters, too. I mentioned in the previous chapter that most of the legal benefits and prerogatives of marriage have to do with creating rights of kinship and helping to cope with the burdens of caregiving; and so they do. Individually, each legal provision underscores that the spouses' job is to be there for each other. At least as important, however, is what I think of as the metamessage, which the bundle of legal prerogatives brings. You and your partner can go to a lawyer and arrange many (not all!) of the legal ties of marriage, but by delivering the whole package all at once the government signifies that, after your wedding, you are a different kind of person—a married person. It is not just that you have chosen to assume this or that responsibility. You have bought into the whole deal. "Marriage is a life-altering boundary," the law is saying. "You're on one side or the other. And now you have officially crossed over."

Marriage is coercive, but in the best possible way, which is to say, the softest. The reward for marrying successfully is approval and respect; the penalty for failing in marriage is sympathetic disappointment. The days are over when single people hit a low glass ceiling in business or politics, but married people are still often considered to have greater personal stability and social standing. The days are over, too, when single people were objects of pity or scorn ("Poor thing—she'll be an old maid if she doesn't marry soon"); but when Grandma cluck-clucks over a still-unmarried young man, or when Mom says she wishes her daughter would settle down, she is expressing a preference—one which is echoed in a thousand subtle ways throughout society and which produces a gentle but persistent pressure to form and sustain unions. Marriage is not mandatory, and never should be; but it is *expected*. Getting married is the normal thing for adults to do. More than any other action, institution, or designation, it separates the grown-ups from the kids. Divorce is not forbidden and never should be; but it is *sad*. Even in an age of common, sometimes nearly instant divorce, every married couple is aware that, in society's eyes, a divorce, even a necessary divorce, is an occasion for commiseration, a kind of failure. When someone says he just went through a divorce, people's first reaction is, "Gosh, I'm sorry," not "Bully for you!" Such are the external prods and lures which create and sustain marriages: soft enough not to be censorious or oppressive, but strong enough to nudge people toward commitment.

Why the elaborate web of rituals and expectations? Why turn marriage into the Brooklyn Bridge of social engineering? The answer isn't obscure. Committing to the care and comfort of another for life is hard. Some couples can stay in love romantically forever, and good for them. Some people find that devotion and self-abnegation come easy, and they are lucky enough to find partners with the same naturally generous character. Some people have the patience of saints. For most ordinary mortals, however, love and altruism aren't always enough. Community begins where love leaves off. Community—our desire not to disappoint our parents and in-laws and friends, our hunger for status, our concern for reputation—can never make marriage easy; but, for many of us, it does make marriage easier. It reminds spouses, during the rough patches, of what they mean to each other, by reminding them of what their marriage means to the people who love them.

That is why it is entirely appropriate that married people enjoy special social standing. They are doing something which is difficult, and they are doing it not only for their own sake and their children's, but for the good of the community. The community owes them a debt.

————

All great technologies look magical from the outside but turn out, when opened and dissected, to be systems of interdependent and mutually reinforcing mechanisms. The magic is not in the pieces but in the way they work together. A thread is weak, but an integrated system of mutually reinforcing threads—otherwise known as a rope—is strong. Likewise with marriage. At bottom, it is a collection of incentives, working together to reinforce the message that the state of matrimony is a uniquely solemn commitment. (Some would say a holy or sacred commitment: different frame of reference, same idea.)

When two people marry, they are bonded, to begin with, by reciprocal self-interest. Each wants love and stability from the other, and must give a commitment in order to receive one in return. Then come law and public policy, which reinforce reciprocity by conditioning a bundle of prerogatives on the couple's commitment. The rights are tied to the responsibilities: to get one, you need to promise to live up to the other. Legally speaking, getting out of the deal can be expensive, time-consuming, and messy, even if the experience is not also emotionally bruising. The knowledge that they cannot count on casually getting out deters people from casually going in. Then come social expectations, in the form of custom, convention, ritual, and the various ways by which the people in the couple's world express their interest in the marriage. Each incentive is important in its own right, but the most significant thing is the way reciprocity, law, and community reinforce each other to create a field of force around the couple: a magnetism, and also a mystique. Marriage becomes an awesome commitment, not just a lifestyle but a way of life.

Marriage depends on the power we give it. It, too, has needs; and its needs, too, interlock and reinforce each other. To work best, marriage needs to be understood as a special commitment and a distinct phase of life. Brides and grooms must feel that when they say the vows they are not just reciting poetry but crossing a boundary. To achieve that effect, marriage needs clarity, uniqueness, and universality. We can't confer a special status on marriage unless we know who is married. We can't preserve marriage's mystique if marrying is just one of many arrangements people make to express their fondness for each other or to link their bank accounts. And we can't preserve marriage as a norm if only some people can marry. If you want to damage marriage, then blur its boundaries, surround it with competitors, and riddle it with carve-outs and exceptions. While you are at it, unbundle the rights from the responsibilities. Give some people the prerogatives of marriage without asking them to make the Big Commitment, and give other people the burdens of marriage without giving them its special status. Just for good measure, leave people unsure exactly who is married and who is not.

And that, at last, brings us back to same-sex marriage, and the proposed alternatives to it.

———

If you are married, a question: How do you know?

Seriously. Suppose someone showed up on your doorstep and demanded that you prove you are married. How would you do it?

You might say your spouse is the only person you ever sleep with; but what if the two of you no longer have sex, or what if one of you has fooled around? You could say you live together, but so do many people who are not married. You could point to your children, if you have any, but nowadays many unmarried couples have children. You could proclaim your love for your spouse—if you still love your spouse—but that would not prove anything, either. You could ask your friends and neighbors to vouch for you, but how do they know? You could point to the ring on your finger, or go find some wedding pictures, but—well, you get the point. Imagine what a time-consuming nuisance it would be to assemble a dossier to prove that you and your spouse have made a special, lifelong commitment. Much easier to do something else: have the inquirer check the records at the courthouse, which will indicate right away that you are married.

If marriage is to be a special promise which brings special status, people need to know who has made the promise and who deserves the status. We need a standard way to know who is married and who isn't. Civil marriage provides that standard. In America, without an established church, *only* civil marriage can provide it.

When you get a marriage license, you do more than pick up a piece of paper. You cross the line into a new relationship not only with your partner but with the state and, through the state, society. There is, of course, that big basket of legal prerogatives which, all of a sudden, you qualify for. Moreover, you have entered a legal relationship which is complicated and difficult to get out of—at least if your spouse is disinclined to make it easy. Moreover, if you and your spouse come into conflict over money or children (among other things), you both give the courts jurisdiction over your personal affairs. That piece of paper from the government turns out not to be just a piece of paper at all. Rather, it signifies that the state now views you in an entirely different way.

This is the demarcating function of civil marriage. Nowadays few weddings are alike (just recall some of the matrimonial readings you may have heard—or, maybe better yet, don't). No two marriages are alike, either. And here is the beauty part: thanks to secular marriage, they do not have to be alike. We can all have our own religions and ceremonies and marriages; we can get married on roller skates while chanting karmic mantras; but by seeking and recognizing state authority for our vows, we signal to each other and to the world that we really are married. The license is more than a handy one-stop way to draw up a complicated contract, although it certainly is that. It is also a universally recognized sign which says: "These people have made the ultimate commitment, so treat them accordingly."

In the larger scheme of things, civil marriage is a fairly new development. E. J. Graff, in *What Is Marriage For?*, traces secular authority over marriage to the Protestant Reformation of the early sixteenth century. Before that, formal marriage was essentially a private transaction, largely managed by landed families as a matter of business. In Europe, not until A.D. 774 did the Church begin to get involved, and another five hundred years went by before it "came up with a marriage liturgy and imposed its new and radical rules—the ballooning incest rules, the one-man-one-marriage rule, and most controversial, the girl-must-consent rule—on the powerful clans." Even so, for some time the Church held that people could marry by exchanging vows in private. That, of course, created certain problems. A father would line up a nice husband for his daughter, only to have some bumpkin come out of the woodwork alleging that he and she had secretly exchanged vows some time before. To cope with clandestine marriage, the Church determined that marriage required a formal announcement in advance (the posting of the banns) and a ceremony before priest and witnesses. Even so, notes Graff, in the Church's eyes the private exchange of vows made for a *valid* marriage—the two hearts had been conjoined—if not a *licit* one.

Most people still married privately, and "private marriage created public mess." Graff continues:

> Across Europe people didn't know whether they were married or un-, what with engagements or annulments tied up in court for years; secret vows and seductions that might or might not be binding for life; priests paying annual fees for concubines who were not wives; and of course the proliferation of marriage taxes for dispensations, pronouncements, annulments, and what have you. And so in swept the Protestants, with their ferocious appetite for sexual order.

They insisted that marriage be not a mystical sacrament before God but "a secular status conferred by an outside authority. No Protestant group had the power to control that public recognition. . . . So they handed off marriage to their running-mates for power, the rising nation-states." That was in the early 1500s. In some places, such as England, another two centuries would pass before secular authority really established itself; and in America, with its frontier culture, common-law marriage persisted into the nineteenth century. If a pair of settlers in the wilderness looked and acted married for a long time, married they were.

Then came a final twist. Having got into the marriage business, secular authority partly backed out of it. At first it regulated neither the boundaries nor the structure of marriage; then it regulated both, with laws establishing that, for example, the man was head of the family and effectively owned his wife; and then, in the modern era, the state took to regulating the boundaries of marriage *instead* of the structure. Couples today are entirely free to decide how they want to organize, and behave in, their marriages; yet it is the state alone which signals whether they *are* married.

Standards without content, boundaries without rules: How could that be possible? The power of the marriage license comes not from its instructions (it bears none) but from its entanglements and entitlements. Above all, people take the license seriously because of the weight that other people give it. The marriage certificate is a kind of currency, like paper money. We value it because others do. So there you have another of those elegant reinforcement loops which make marriage such an ingenious technology.

What would happen, then, if we subtracted the state from the equation, getting it out of the marriage business? Individuals, religious organizations, government agencies, employers, and communities would need to sort out for themselves whom to treat as married. Pretty much every employer that provides health benefits makes them available to spouses. Without the government's clear signal, how would employers know who qualifies? They would have to set their own standards for marriage and demand that employees prove they qualify (intrusive and contentious), or just take everybody's word for it (potentially expensive and an invitation to abuse), or withdraw spousal benefits altogether (one less incentive for people to get and stay married). Ordinary people would sometimes be at sea, too. John and Sue next door seem to be married, but I'm not sure. Is it polite to ask? They don't seem to act married, so how do I treat them if they say they are? People can be shrewd judges of relationships, and even if marriage were privatized, we would often be able to distinguish between the committed couples and the casual ones. Religious weddings and private ceremonies would still carry weight. But instead of sharing a common marital currency, we would be reduced to barter: case-by-case determination, with all the fuzziness, arbitrariness, and unfairness the practice would entail. ("Dear Abby: My company claims I haven't been living with my partner long enough to count as married. What do I do?")

I now make bold to introduce what I'll designate Rule 1 of marriage: "If you want the benefits of marriage, *get married*." This is the rule which ties the benefits to the burdens and the rights to the responsibilities. To make it work, one has to know who actually *is* married. Civil marriage, by setting clear and widely accepted boundaries without bossing anyone around or throwing anyone in jail, has proved itself to be one of the most effective government programs of all time. Marriage is the last thing the government should get out of.

―――――

The key is to link the benefits to the burdens. It is not good for marriage if a large group of people are asked to accept the burdens without receiving the benefits. That, of course, is the current status of homosexuals, but I'll return to that subject in chapter 5. Here, let's flip the coin over. What happens if we start giving people the benefits without requiring them to accept the burdens? That is marriage-lite.

Domestic-partner programs, as they are most often called (although the ones that more closely resemble marriage are sometimes called civil unions), are hard to generalize about, because they can take many forms. That, in fact, is one of the problems with them, and is a key way in which they differ from matrimony: whereas civil marriage is a standard package whose terms are well understood and widely accepted, a domestic-partner program can be anything its sponsor says it is. The Human Rights Campaign, a leading gay-rights group, counts an employer as having a domestic-partner program if it provides health benefits to employees' unmarried partners. Employers may, of course, provide more, or less, or nothing—nothing being still the norm, even though partner benefits are growing more common.

Who qualifies as a partner, as opposed to, say, a roommate? There is no standard definition. To cope with that problem, two states and more than fifty cities and counties have established some kind of domestic-partner registry. In some cases—not all, since, again, there is no standard—the registries "allow same-sex couples to obtain certain rights and benefits traditionally associated with marriage, such as hospital and jail visitation, child-care leave, and certain parental rights," reports the Human Rights Campaign. Employers may choose to accept public registration, where available, as proof of being coupled, and they can also set terms of their own. American Airlines, for instance, requires that domestic-partner beneficiaries "reside together in the same permanent residence and have lived in a spouse-like relationship for at least six consecutive months"; enrollees can get medical, life-insurance, and travel benefits for their partners. Vermont and California have enacted broad partner programs that look a lot like marriage, although they confer none of the many federal benefits. Like marriage, these state-recognized unions can be fairly hard to get out of, requiring divorce proceedings. On the other hand, many partner programs can be terminated virtually at the drop of a hat, sometimes on the say-so of only one partner. (Until California reformed its program recently, either party could unilaterally mail in a form saying, "I, the undersigned, do declare that Former Partner: _____ and I are no longer Domestic Partners." No fee, just use certified mail.) And many programs merely offer piecemeal benefits for couples in particular situations, as when New York State granted special health benefits to partners of firefighters who died at the World Trade Center.

So there is quite a spectrum. Marriage-lite can be a lot of things. The one and practically only thing it reliably is not, indeed, is marriage. However close a domestic-partner program may come legally, it is no substitute for the genuine article.

That is because marriage is more than a package of benefits which happen to have been bundled together for convenience's sake. It adds value by bringing to bear the weight of social expectations that to marry is to commit. Everyone knows to expect married couples to be there for each other. Will people know what to expect of a domestic partnership, that newfangled invention of political activists and human-resources departments? Marriage-lite may have all of the bonding power of marriage, or it may have only some, or it may have none, depending on how seriously society and the partners take it. For myself, I cannot imagine my mother sobbing with joy and relief as she says, "Thank goodness, Jon has finally found a domestic partner."

The health benefits that come with domestic partnership, of course, are a useful and important thing—precious, if your partner has diabetes or HIV or cancer. A gay man I know is looking after a dying partner who needs constant care at home. He covers the night shift himself, but his employer, a university, provides daytime nursing through its domestic-partner program, a godsend. Without health benefits in cases like this, the healthy partner may have to quit work to be a full-time nurse, or the couple may wind up on Medicaid or charity, or the ailing partner may suffer from inadequate care, or the stress of improvising may prove emotionally and financially overwhelming. If the only two choices were between domestic-partner programs for gay couples and nothing at all, I would certainly take the domestic-partner programs. One reason is practical: it is in society's interest to promote settled relationships among homosexuals, and society is better off promoting marriage-lite, which has at least some shape and structure and promise of commitment, than cohabitation. Another reason is moral: to require homosexual couples to get along without any of the benefits of marriage is callous. For most gay people, as for most straight people, a long-term partnership (or the aspiration to one) is an indispensable element of the good life, and so it is unfair and inhumane to tell homosexuals: "Sure, a life partner is important; and sure, a partnership is a lot harder to sustain if you lack social support and legal tools and have to start from scratch each time in a lawyer's office; but that's too bad—no matter how devoted you are to your partner, no matter how many bedpans you empty in times of illness or how many extra jobs you take to pay your other half's emergency bills, in the eyes of the law, you two will never be more than shacked up."

For those reasons, I believe that if homosexuals are not to be allowed to marry, the decent and smart thing is to establish partnership programs. But I make this statement with trepidation. For gay people, civil unions and the like are a seat at the back of the bus, a badge of inferiority pinned on every same-sex union; but second best is better than nothing at all, from a gay point of view. From both a gay *and* a straight point of view, however, marriage-lite is a distant second choice. Quite possibly, domestic-partner arrangements will do little more than recognize and subsidize existing relationships. Marriage is something else again. It defines new relationships and, on a good day, transforms old ones.

Marriage-lite is not a true substitute for marriage, because it is not the same thing. And that, at bottom, is exactly the point: many people believe that same-sex relationships are different from opposite-sex relationships, and inferior to them, and that public policy should maintain the distinction. People who believe this are not necessarily bigoted or cruel. They might say that being homosexual is not as good as being heterosexual. If you take this point of view, the ABM pact must seem a no-brainer: reserve the special designation for the special relationship. What you may be failing to consider is how the ABM pact will backfire—is in fact already backfiring—against marriage.

———

Look around. Who, in America, supports the creation of domestic-partner programs? Many moderates who cannot bring themselves to endorse same-sex marriage, of course, but also an outspoken assortment of leftists, some gay and some straight but most of them radical (and proud of it). Even though they usually favor same-sex marriage on equity grounds, they are ambivalent about it as a policy. What they really like are civil unions. "Forget Marriage. Give Us Benefits!" was how the *New York Times* put it in a 2003 headline, summarizing the opinion of a letter writer who said that "broad civil-unions legislation is both more inclusive and more achievable" than marriage. Now, that seems curious. What is it these people see which the rest of us may be over-looking?

Well, they are no friends of marriage, for the most part. They view it as stifling if they are libertines, archaic if they are radicals, patriarchal if they are feminists, and often as all of the above. Most of them would say marriage takes much too narrow a view of what constitutes a family. The privileging of marriage—the special standing marriage enjoys—is precisely what they oppose. They would rather see a thousand flowers bloom. And, to them, domestic partnerships are the gateway to the garden.

There are two ways to erode and perhaps eliminate the special status of matrimony. One is to take away its unique government endorsement by getting the state out of the marriage business. Politically, however, that is a nonstarter; and, in any case, the alternatives-to-marriage movement believes that the state should support and subsidize relationships—but not only *marital* rela-tionships. So the ticket (goes the argument) is to extend the benefits of marriage to the unmarried. Give the benefits to com-mitted partners of whatever gender. Give them to seniors and their caregivers. Maybe even give them to—here it comes—groups. The alternatives-to-marriage movement wants the gov-ernment to stop picking and choosing among relationships and lifestyles. Domestic-partnership programs are a foot in the door.

I should stress that there are at least as many heterosexual advocates of the position I have just described as there are homo-sexual ones. I should also stress that not all of them are antimar-riage, at least not in their own eyes. The real target here is what Katha Pollitt, writing in *The Nation* magazine in 1996, called "the socio-marital order": society's systemic preference for marriage. If some people want to get married, more power to them. It is just that there should be alternatives for people who don't want to get married. The goal, wrote Pollitt, consists in "diminishing the increasingly outmoded privileged status of marriage and sharing out its benefits along different, more egalitarian lines."

Well, marriage can be a royal pain, no two ways about it. "Marriage will not only open up to gay men and lesbians whole new vistas of guilt, frustration, claustrophobia, bewilderment, declining self-esteem, unfairness, and sorrow," wrote Pollitt, "it will offer them the opportunity to prolong this misery by tormenting each other in court." In 1998 a heterosexual man, who was living with a woman to whom he was not married, sued his company, Bell Atlantic, for the right to be included in the company's partner-benefits program. His legal filing complained that Bell Atlantic's policy was "imposing burdens on the employee such as the need for health tests, the need for a marriage ceremony, and the need for a divorce proceeding to terminate the relationship." What a bother! Hawaii passed a domestic-partner law, by contrast, which allowed the "reciprocal beneficiary" relationship to be terminated by either partner without the other's consent or even knowledge. That program, by the way, was open to both gay and straight couples.

It certainly would be convenient if your employer and society and the law simply provided recognition and benefits for whatever relationship you happened to be having. Writing in 2003 in the *Village Voice*, Richard Goldstein argued that "civil unions present a model that can be broadly applied":

> Down the road we may see groups of people sharing the custody of children, or geriatric communes seeking a legal tie. Each of these contingencies will involve its own process of agitation, and it will be up to society to accept or reject each claim. But the result could be a menu of possibilities, ranging from trial unions to so-called covenant marriages that are very difficult to leave. People may elect to pass from one category to another as their attitudes change. This begins to look like the kind of world radicals want to see—a world of choice.

That sounds sweet. Instead of having to decide whether to jump across a boundary society sets for you (marriage), you could just pass from one sort of thing to the next, with society adjusting to whatever boundaries you set as you go along. Wouldn't it be nice if there were a halfway house (or a halfway group house)? A way to get health insurance without having to say "till death us do part"?

Actually, a lot of people, gay and straight, would like a halfway house: or, to be more blunt about it, a free ride. Throughout most of history, society has been smart enough to deny it to them. For some people, marrying is a dream, and nothing less will do; but for others, the decision to wed is a leap in the dark, a jump off the high dive. Today those people tend to cohabit, and, over time, many of them work up the nerve to tie the knot. But that is partly because, from cohabitation, there is no way up but to marriage. It's up or out—often out, given that cohabitations are less stable than marriages.

Granted, to enact civil unions would not be merely to subsidize cohabitation. Because—depending on their design—civil unions may confer some of the legal entitlements and entanglements that marriage does, they have bonding effects. Lately the trend has been to start adding legal responsibilities to formal partner programs—a welcome development. Nonetheless, marriage-lite is an arrow aimed at the very heart of Rule 1. ("If you want the benefits of marriage, *get married*.") To whatever extent they mimic marriage, domestic-partner programs send the message that, from the law's and thus society's point of view, marriage is no longer unique. On the other hand, to whatever extent they fall short of marriage, domestic-partner programs fail to give same-sex couples what they need. The dilemma is elemental.

———

That would not be such a problem if domestic-partner benefits were limited to homosexuals, who, after all, can't marry. The benefits should be so limited. The question is: Can they be? The answer is, generally, no.

Say you are a corporate human-resources executive. Your business has established a domestic-partner program for gay employees. One day you receive a delegation of straight workers, maybe under the auspices of the union. They say they have partners but happen not to be married. They want partner benefits, too.

"Well," you say, "you have the option of marrying."

You're right, of course. But you already sense you're on thin ice. The answer—you can see it coming—is indignant. "Who are you to tell us how to run our personal lives? You mean that, to get equal treatment, we have to sit here and explain the many good reasons why we have chosen not to marry? Since when did working here mean letting you invade our privacy and judge our relationships?" You can see where this conversation goes. Gays lose partner benefits or, more likely, straights get them.

Matters are no different in the public sector. Politicians follow the votes, and most of the votes in America belong to heterosexuals. When gays get a benefit, straights want it, too, and there are many more of them. Consider the political calculus. On the far left, reformers want to subsidize alternatives to marriage. In the middle, unmarried straights like the idea of new benefits (why not?). Gay groups figure the surest way to get and keep partner programs is to give the straight majority a stake in them. The far right's main concern is blocking partner programs for homosexuals. The only constituency for restricting marriage-lite to homosexuals is the presumably small number of people who understand the principle at stake and are willing to fall on their swords for it.

No surprise, then, to learn that most partner programs in America are in fact open to both same-sex and opposite-sex couples—about two-thirds of them, according to the Human Rights Campaign, which keeps tabs on public and private programs. As of the end of 2002, nine states, the District of Columbia, and 140 municipalities and other local government agencies offered domestic-partner benefits (including at least health insurance); 70 percent of those programs were open to both gay and straight couples. Among the *Fortune* 500 companies, 154 offered domestic-partner programs, of which just over 60 percent were open to straight couples. The Human Rights Campaign finds that the number of employers providing domestic-partner health benefits has been growing by roughly 20 percent a year since 1999, and about two-thirds of the programs are straight-inclusive.

Moreover, political pressures being what they are, some jurisdictions have passed "equal benefits ordinances" *requiring* that partner programs be "nondiscriminatory" (that is, open to heterosexual couples), and court and administrative rulings tug in the same direction. In 1996, the city of Oakland, California, set up a gays-only partnership program for city workers, and the city tried to hold the line, but it was finally forced to admit unmarried heterosexuals when the state labor commissioner ruled that excluding them constituted illegal discrimination. In Santa Barbara, the city attorney likewise opined that gays-only benefits were illegal, and the city extended its program to include opposite-sex unmarried couples.

As partner programs multiply and lose their exotic air, more heterosexuals will sign up for them. According to the Human Rights Campaign, the number of people on the health-benefits roster grows by 1 percent when partner benefits are granted only to gay couples but by 3 percent when the benefits are opened to straight couples—suggesting that roughly two-thirds of the participants are heterosexual. That should not be surprising. There are many more straights than gays. So what we are talking about is not a hypothetical slippery slope toward heterosexual marriage-lite. The slide is already under way, here and now.

In response, conservatives might say, "You're right! There is only one solution. Stop the partner programs. The way to protect marriage has got to be: no same-sex marriage, no domestic-partner programs, no nothing. Gays will just have to cope on their own."

No good. Worse, in fact. Domestic-partner programs are not the only competitor to marriage, nor are they even the most important. More common and more destabilizing—and open to gays and straights alike—is cohabitation. If gay couples are denied both legal marriage and domestic partnership, they will just live together outside marriage. They will come to the office holiday party together and house-shop together and entertain together and, perhaps, raise children together; all of which will bolster the status of cohabitation as a respectable, and in many ways equivalent, alternative to marriage. Over time, as society makes room for unmarried but devoted same-sex couples, custom and law will provide cohabitants with many of marriage's benefits—only without the bother of formal commitment, legal responsibilities, or a messy divorce. Many heterosexual couples, including many with children, will be only too happy to take the deal. Just such a trend is already well along in Canada and a number of European countries, where the legal and social boundaries between cohabitation and marriage are quickly blurring.

There is no way around the problem here. Conservatives seem to believe that, if they stop same-sex marriage, they will stop all sorts of other gay-friendly change along with it. They talk as if the alternative to same-sex marriage were to go back to 1950, or at least 1980. With or without gay marriage, however, the world is changing and will continue to change. Every day more homosexuals are coming out to their friends and families, and so every day more heterosexuals number homosexuals among their loved ones. Not many Americans—not a majority, in any case—wish for their sons and daughters and sisters and brothers and friends a partnerless life in a sexual underworld; they want gay people, like straight people, to have a clean shot at happiness, including partnership. They see successful same-sex relationships, which are not so freakish or unhealthy after all, and they think: "Well, if Mary gets sick, why *shouldn't* Sue be able to visit her in the hospital?" They say: "Surely telling a whole group of people they can't marry is a severe imposition. If we're going to exclude gays from marriage in the name of a larger social good, shouldn't we at least try to do what we can for them? And doesn't encouraging them to form unions and settle down make more sense from society's point of view than just pretending they don't exist and hoping they never get sick?" It is not the "homosexual lobby" which is nudging the public toward acknowledging and supporting same-sex relationships, nor is it any kind of degeneracy or moral dumbing-down. Just the opposite: it is the decency and common sense of ordinary Americans.

The trend toward social recognition of same-sex couples is past stopping. The pending question today is whether to bestow society's blessings on marriage or on something else—marriage-lite or socially approved cohabitation or, most likely, both. Already, in America, if you want to get together with someone, and depending on where you live or work, you can have cohabitation, employer domestic-partner benefits, public domestic-partner benefits, marriage, or even covenant marriage (a version of marriage which is harder to get into and out of). At this rate, marriage may become merely an item on a mix-and-match menu of lifestyle options, a truffle in the candy box. It might even become the preserve of the old-fashioned. "Oh, you're getting a *traditional* marriage? Isn't that charming!"

Marriage is durable and, one way or another, will survive, even in a world of proliferating alternatives. What seems incontestable, however, is that empowering a bunch of competitors cannot do marriage any good, especially if the competitors offer most of the benefits with fewer of the burdens. If marriage's self-styled defenders continue along the ABM path toward making wedlock just one of many "partnership choices" (and not necessarily the most attractive), they will look back one day and wonder what they could possibly have been thinking when they undermined marriage in order to save it from homosexuals.

Obviously, there is another path forward, one which reinforces rather than corrodes Rule 1. Let everybody marry.

3

How Gays Will Benefit

Same-sex marriage is a win-win-win. It is the trifecta of modern social policy. In this and the next two chapters, I will explain why.

I would have thought, and so might you, that a chapter explaining why gay marriage is good for gays would be easy to write. Isn't it obvious? A whole bunch of benefits. Full legal equality (from a gay observer's point of view). A new level of social acceptance. What's not to like? Among gay Americans, the marriage-rights movement goes back to May 1970, less than a year after the Stonewall riots in New York put gay rights on the map. Jack Baker and Mike McConnell, with their minister's blessing, applied for a marriage license in Hennepin County, Minnesota. When they were turned down, they filed suit. They lost, and so did a succession of other gay claimants, until 1993, when Hawaii's Supreme Court ruled that the state couldn't deny a marriage license to Ninia Baehr and Genora Dancel, a lesbian couple, without giving a compelling reason. In those days, gay-movement leaders were often reluctant to focus on marriage when so many battles for antidiscrimination laws—the movement's traditional civil rights priority—remained to be won. From the beginning, it has been the homosexual rank and file, the man and woman in the street and the pew, who have pressed for marriage.

The benefits of marriage, then, have long been apparent to gay people. Not all the benefits, however, are as obvious as the ones we mostly hear about. Marriage not only blesses our unions; it changes them. It changes us. It closes the book on gay liberation: it liberates us from liberation, if you will. And that is good.

But start with the obvious stuff, because it is important.

———

My friend Brian is a lawyer. "When Tom's mother died," he told me (Tom was his partner of six years at the time), "I had a trial scheduled for the day of the funeral. I had to move for a continuance, but how do you ask a very conservative judge in Pensacola to delay trial because your boyfriend's mother just died?" His side did get the continuance, but if it had been his mother-in-law who had died, Brian reflected, the delay might not have been an issue.

A small thing. Or perhaps not so small. Perhaps large. Being there when your partner is sick or in trouble, or when your mother-in-law is dying, is what marriage is for. Not infrequently, the lack of marriage's kin-creating tools can cripple commitment when the need is greatest. I logged onto the Web site of Lambda Legal, a gay-rights organization, and found no shortage of wrenching stories.

> Ronnie in New York City developed a grave illness and needed her partner of over twenty years, Elaine, to assist her in getting to medical appointments. Ronnie would suffer blackouts walking in the street. Elaine requested family medical leave from her employer to cover the periodic appointments, but the employer said no because Ronnie was not a "spouse." Elaine had to turn to friends and neighbors to cover the appointments, and worried about how long the help would last.

> Bill and Robert considered themselves "soulmates." When Robert fell fatally ill, the admitting Maryland hospital knew

through his accompanying medical records—and Bill's statements to hospital staff—that Bill was Robert's family and legal agent for health care decisions. But the hospital blocked any communication between them, saying that only "family" were allowed access to patients. Bill was forced to watch with mounting anguish and humiliation as families of other patients arrived and quickly were escorted in to see their loved ones. Robert slipped into unconsciousness, alone and without comfort, support, and solace during his final hours. He never saw or spoke with Bill before his death.

Ivonne and Jeanette have two children who lived with them in a studio apartment in a subsidized housing project in New York. The landlord denied their application for a larger apartment because the two women were not married and therefore not considered a "family." Then the landlord turned around and tried to evict them for "overcrowding" because the studio was too small for a couple with two children. . . . [T]he moms had to find a lawyer to protect them from eviction because they could not get married.

For 28 years in rural Washington, Frank and Bob shared their lives and home, and built a business together. When Bob died suddenly without a will, his relatives—the legal heirs—swept in demanding that Frank move out of the house and turn over the business and all the couple's other assets to them. If they succeed in court, Frank will be penniless.

That is life without marriage: capricious, insecure, sometimes pointlessly cruel. As I sat down to write this chapter, I found this E-mail of the Day on the Web site of the gay journalist and blogger Andrew Sullivan:

I just completed thirty years working for the Department of Defense, the last fourteen years spent in ensuring our missile defense systems are properly tested. Yet, as I look forward to retirement eligibility in 1,047 days, I know that I cannot include my husband on my health insurance policies or as a beneficiary for my pension, as can my straight married co-workers. This grinds on me daily. We spent several thousand dollars last year redoing wills, forming revocable trusts, establishing various powers of attorney, etc. That helps, but nothing short of full marriage will allow the health and pension benefits that I believe we deserve just as much as my colleagues who take them for granted. Of course, my family doesn't matter, as our opponents say; we're just in it for the sex. (I think I remember what that is.) No matter that my husband's bedridden, Alzheimer's-afflicted mother has lived in our house for the last two years; we're just in it for the sex. (Try changing the diaper of a 120-pound, uncooperative woman; babies are nothing in comparison.)

The "benefits that I believe we deserve." The words may sound whiny and demanding, but really what the writer speaks of is not so much the benefits he deserves as the responsibilities he has undertaken. He and his partner have come to depend on each other, have striven to be dependable, yet still lack the security which any pair of flighty Las Vegas newlyweds takes for granted. "Benefits," in fact, is not the right word for what is at issue here. Gay partners are not asking to get something; they are asking to be able to give something: a workday to tend to a sick partner, a hand at a mother-in-law's hospital bedside, a shared home, a bequest. Gay people's request to have their relationships "affirmed," "recognized," "supported" may sound as if they want a trophy. What they need, however, is not a pat on the back but solid ground under their feet. They are asking that the law reinforce rather than undermine their devotion.

In federal law (according to the General Accounting Office), civil marriage is a gateway to 1,138 benefits, rights, and obligations. States provide many more: 210 legal rights and responsibilities in the District of Columbia, for example, according to Richard

Rosendall of Washington's Gay and Lesbian Activists Alliance, which took the trouble to count. Kin creation is a complicated business. Without the toolbox of marriage, spousehood is a legal improvisation, and without spousehood, life itself is a kind of improvisation. No wonder gay people have been trying to get married almost from the day they stopped letting themselves be dragged away in handcuffs. They wanted to be married because—well, who would want to live life without marriage?

———

I don't mean that everyone needs to be married, or that anyone who is not married leads a blighted life. I mean that life is not the same without any prospect of marriage, without any hope of marriage, yesterday and tomorrow and forever. When homosexuals ask to marry, they are not just asking for a legal stamp of approval on the life they have. They are asking for the prospect of a different and (in more cases than not) better kind of life: a life blessed with the physical and moral goods that marriage brings. They are asking, really, for a better kind of love.

Here I may be on thin ice with gay readers who will protest that there is nothing wrong with gay love as it is. In one sense, they are absolutely right. Homosexual love is natural and essential *for homosexuals,* just as heterosexual love is natural and essential for heterosexuals. I mean something else. Sex, love, and marriage go together. Each works better in conjunction with the other two; each gives shape and direction to the others. Sex without love and love (at least romantic love) without sex both tend to be hollow, unstable, and difficult to integrate into a healthy emotional life. And marriage is just as important as the other two. From early adolescence, the prospect of marriage and the expectation of marriage (and the knowledge that society expects marriage) condition the meaning of love. Every kiss, every passion, from the first crush and the first date, has a different, deeper meaning in the context of possible marriage.

Marriage gives love a direction, a calling. It promises that love can lead somewhere, to a purpose higher than oneself. It also gives purpose to sex by making it potentially a union of lives rather than just of bodies. How often have you heard someone say, "We broke up because he (or she) wanted more than I was ready to give"? Translation: the sex stopped when one partner realized it wasn't leading anywhere. (Gay people have that same conversation all the time, by the way.) The prospect of marriage makes some people less promiscuous. It makes others *more* promiscuous, at least temporarily (what used to be called "sowing one's wild oats"). Either way, however, it creates stakes for sex and a destination for love. If love were a car and sex the fuel, marriage would be the road ahead.

The prospect of marriage is thus the prospect of something I never thought, when I was growing up, I could have: an integrated life, with love, sex, and marriage in harmony. Of course I am not suggesting that two people can always live in harmony; not for nothing did Golde describe her love as twenty-five years of fighting with Tevye. I mean two souls bonded in each other's eyes and together clasped to their community's bosom. I mean the embrace of a warm body on a cold night, and the comfort of tomorrow's reconciliation after today's fight, and the reassurance of the law's and society's affirmation that the bond is bigger than the two partners.

A lot of unmarried people, including a lot of gay people, will say they can achieve real commitment and real love (and real screaming matches) in their relationships, and they are right. In the world's eyes, though, only legal marriage makes kinship out of love. Kissing your high-school sweetheart while knowing that someday he could be your domestic partner or live-in lover is not the same as looking ahead to marriage. Moreover, only marriage—nothing else—has the power to end, for homosexuals, the Long Dark Age.

———

In the latter half of the thirteenth century, European society embarked on a campaign against homosexuality which lasted until just a few decades ago. Things got better and worse here and there, but the fundamentals remained broadly the same. For heterosexuals, sex and love and marriage were all interwoven. For homosexuals, they were all forbidden.

Forbidden, however, in different ways and degrees. Sex was tolerable, up to a point. It had to be secret, or you had to be well connected to get away with it, or you had to confess to it and promise never to do it again, or it could be written off as a burst of coltish high spirits. And, of course, it happened all the time. Inevitably a sexual underworld emerged, a place of squalor and exploitation and coldly mechanical sex, but also of companionship and solidarity and fleeting human warmth. Homosexuals learned to live in two worlds at once. They pretended to be heterosexual, and, if they were lucky, heterosexuals pretended to believe them.

Love, by contrast, was a more serious offense. The need for the touch and affection of another of the same sex—not just horniness but emotional need—made you one of *them*, a perv, a fruit, a queer, something shameful or sinful or sick or all of the above and more besides. You could have sex, up to a point, provided you did not love. And, although it was not advisable, you could also love, up to a quite limited point, provided you did not have sex. The authorities knew perfectly well how sex and love reinforce each other to create an emotionally integrated life, and that was what they were determined should not happen.

One thing, of course, you could not do at all. You couldn't marry the person you loved. The mere suggestion would have been unthinkable.

Because they go naturally together, sex, love, and marriage are difficult to separate. Prying them apart required a regime of moral and physical terror. If a homosexual showed his true colors, outside of certain protective cosmopolitan circles, he could expect to be idled, shunned, confined, medicated, beaten, or killed. (Life was somewhat easier for lesbians because it was widely assumed that no such thing as lesbianism could exist.) To this day, there are streets in the United States where I hesitate to hold hands with my partner, for fear of the car that stops and disgorges young men with baseball bats.

Adding a kind of intellectual insult to spiritual and physical injury, the Long Dark Age never bothered to provide homosexuals with a coherent account of their shame. They were warped, sick, perverts, diseased; yet they were also somehow culpable for their own malady. Homosexuals, it was presumed, could be heterosexuals if they tried harder—only everybody knew that, really, a queer was always a queer. In principle, all of God's children were sinners and all could be redeemed, but in practice homosexuals were beyond the pale and written off. Was the condition a disease or a crime? Was the offense being or doing? In fact, the offense and the condition were whatever served conveniently to justify revilement. The sex-love-marriage triangle embodied a theory of the way human beings can, by harmonizing the three, live well. The Long Dark Age smashed the theory where homosexuals were concerned but did not replace it with any other. No matter which way the homosexual turned, there was no path to the good life. The regime was not systematic or sensible; rather, it was a kind of lunacy. For many people, I suspect, the lunacy was worse than the terror. There was no rhyme or reason; you just hoped they didn't come to get you.

If you demur and feel that I exaggerate—that my description of the Long Dark Age is a touch melodramatic—I concur, up to a point. Despite it all, many homosexuals managed to lead fruitful lives. As always, for every dose of terror there was a gesture of compassion. To speak of a Long Dark Age, though, gets the spirit and sweep of the antihomosexual fervor about right. The repression went on for centuries, it seemed certain never to end, and although some people coped, none escaped.

In the United States, cycles turned, rhythms swung. Some periods were better, some worse. The 1940s and 1950s were especially bad. And then, when the excesses of the 1950s led to gay resistance and rebellion, the planet turned and daylight came. The 1960s brought sexual freedom and personal autonomy to society at large, and with it came gay liberation. Homosexuals began creeping out of their closets and blinking in the sun, and as more of them emerged, they started to make their case and press their claims. America, a country with its heart in the right place if ever there was one, changed. Sodomy laws, vice squads, court-martials, and the rest of the apparatus of terror declined toward disuse (although, make no mistake, prosecutors can still make plenty of trouble for homosexuals, and sodomy laws died only in 2003). Gay bashing, while still common, fell into disrepute. Intellectual opinion rejected the Long Dark Age with a vengeance. In the heady climate of the 1960s and 1970s, gay liberation was just one tile in the liberationist (some would say libertine) mosaic. The Long Dark Age was over!

Only it wasn't. Not altogether. People—not just gay people, but many people—had free love and free sex, but they forgot about marriage, or, if they thought about it, repudiated it as a cog in the machinery of repression. Emerging from a world of utter repression into a world of unprecedented freedom, many gay people (and plenty of nongays) threw restraint to the wind. Having relied on the sexual underworld for support and human contact through the dark years, many homosexuals glorified the underworld as their salvation and mistook it for home. "I can still make myself faintly feel the delicious nausea of initiation terror which Christopher felt as Wystan [W. H. Auden] pushed back the heavy leather door curtain of a boy bar called the Cosy Corner and led the way inside," Christopher Isherwood wrote (in his 1976 memoir, *Christopher and His Kind*) of his first visit, in 1929, to a gay bar. For generations of homosexuals, initiation into the sexual underworld had been the universal rite of passage, a thrilling first taste of a kind of hope and a kind of freedom. Now, with liberation at hand, the bars and bathhouses (sex clubs) seemed the obvious point of entry into a new life.

Even then, many people managed to settle down, and, over time, more did so. Then AIDS broke out, and, in the face of the plague, the so-called gay community became a *real* community, organizing support programs and buddy networks and charities and clinics to take care of people whose own families sometimes shunned them. Countless homosexuals learned to change bedpans, wipe spittle, clean vomit, carry a frail body up a flight of stairs. Americans took notice. This was something different. This was not in the Dark Age script.

So homosexuals probed beyond sex to love. They began to understand that they *could* love, and that their love was in no way a disease, but rather that deprivation of love was the disease; and they discovered in their love a wellspring of devotion. Sex and love: they had made the link.

One link remained, namely marriage. Without marriage, the triangle was incomplete, but nonetheless a surprising number of homosexuals set about acting as if they already were married. Some heterosexuals, their view still clouded by assumptions of the Long Dark Age, regarded same-sex partnerships as parodies of the real thing, but many heterosexuals again took notice. Homosexuals were now probing beyond sex and love; but completing the triangle still seemed, to most heterosexuals, a step too far.

And that is where we are today. Increasingly, homosexuals are ready for marriage; heterosexuals, a step behind, are ready for everything *except* marriage. The Long Dark Age, however attenuated its power, will not end until the triangle is complete, because only then will gays have the prospect of a love which is complete. When that happens, the gay-rights era will be over and the gay-responsibility era will begin.

———

In 2003, President George W. Bush paid a moving visit to a slave quarters on Goree Island, off the coast of Senegal. It was here, through the infamous Door of No Return, where thousands of slaves last set foot on African soil before beginning their months-long sail to America. Bush spoke of the iniquities of the slave trade, the stain on the nation, the depredations visited on the slaves. "In law, they were regarded only as articles of commerce, having no right to travel, or to marry, or to own possessions," he said.

Or to marry. Two classes of person were forbidden to marry: slaves and children. The groups had in common that, in the eyes of the law and of society, they were by nature wards and dependents. My intention, of course, is not to compare the situation of homosexuals in America today with that of slaves two centuries ago. The two are not remotely comparable. The point relates to marriage. For a long time, adulthood has been virtually synonymous with being qualified to take a spouse. Some cultures have married off young children (some still do), but the transaction is more like a sale than a modern marriage. With consent-based marriage came the abolition, in the West, of child betrothal, because consent implies the capacity to make grown-up choices. How do you signal that an adult is still to be considered a child, incompetent and unable to master his impulses? Deny him the right to marry.

Although I doubt that the proscription against same-sex marriage originated with any desire to infantilize homosexuals (until recently, homosexuality as a fundamental orientation was not recognized to exist), today the ban certainly has that effect. Many people, if they had to name one event that marked the full transition to adulthood, would probably identify their wedding. The band on the left fourth finger tells the world: I am entrusted with the care of another. Some married people are immature, and some mature people are unmarried. The law requires proof of age for marriage but not proof of maturity. Nonetheless, in society's eyes, marriage is the passport to adulthood. You are out of your parents' home, mainly independent, mutually self-supporting, and on your way to children, economic security, and solid citizenship.

Gay culture, meaning for the most part gay male culture, has been widely criticized, even by some gay people, for its party mentality. When gay-pride marches looked like underwear parties, when careers took second place to raves, and when an activist wore a T-shirt and leather vest to meet with President Clinton in the Oval Office, the word "mature" did not spring to mind. I need to tread carefully here, because in fact the majority of gay individuals are just as mature as the majority of straight people. It was the culture, with its elevation of play over work and of self-expression over self-discipline and of youth over everything, which seemed to suffer from an advanced case of Peter Pan syndrome.

You could say that homosexual culture was or is too immature to handle marriage, but how can a culture fully grow up if it lacks any hope of marriage? In any case, the culture has already come a long way, in part because of the proliferation of openly gay couples, in part because of the increasing presence of children in gay lives, and in part, sadly, because of the AIDS crisis. Millions of gay people are ready to marry. Quite a number of them are in more stable, more tender unions than some of their straight neighbors. For gay culture and gay self-image, marriage is the last and by far the greatest step toward maturity. Within a generation or so, marriage will mean the end of gay culture as we know it.

No, all the party animals won't turn into stay-at-home spouses overnight. Nor should they. But today's marriageless regime says to gay people: "Settle down, make a home if you like, but don't count on the law for any cooperation. As far as the law is concerned, no matter what you do, you are children, capable of liaisons but not of marriage. So party on!" Not illogically, many gay people respond by concluding: "Some of us form lasting unions, others get high on ecstasy and dance our way from trick to trick. In the law's eyes, they are both just lifestyle choices. So party on!" Marriage says something else altogether. It says: if you will make the commitment, you will receive the legal recognition and special status which only marriage brings. If you assume the responsibilities of adulthood, you will get the prerogatives.

Many gay advocates of same-sex marriage see it merely as a legal issue, a question of equal rights. A few, however, have always viewed marriage not just as a legal option but as a powerful cultural norm—and for that reason they have been uneasy with it, sometimes even opposed to it. They understand that, if marriage is legalized, the last walls of the ghetto will come down. Much of what is unique about gay culture—not all, but much, and particularly at the extremes—is an artifact of marginalization and infantilization. The alienation of sex and love from all hope of marriage is the profoundest element of that marginalization and infantilization. Some of the gay critics of same-sex marriage understand marriage's powers of soft coercion. They understand how social expectations and the pathway toward marriage change not just law but love (and sex). They fear that gay cultural uniqueness will be absorbed and then erased by the "heterosexual lifestyle." I believe that they are largely right, and that gay integration into the mainstream would be, on balance, a good thing. To be homosexual will always entail an element of differentness, cultural and personal, if only because gay people will always be a minority in a straight world. In a world with marriage, however, gay differentness will be an expression of individuality, not of alienation. No doubt, the underground gay culture of the Long Dark Age, and then the sex-is-love, life-is-play culture of the Long Dark Age's aftermath, had their uses. But it is time to move on. Marriage and the prospect of marriage change us, and they do so not by saddling us with a new oppression but by giving us a higher kind of freedom: the freedom to be our best selves. What gay people want and need and deserve is to be able to say, and really mean, the four most ennobling words in the English language: "Will you marry me?"

Gay marriage is not so much a civil rights issue as a civil responsibility issue. If the first "homosexual agenda" focused on gay rights—the right to have sex, the right to walk the streets in safety, the right to keep a job—the second focuses on gay responsibilities: marriage, military service, the rearing and mentoring of the young. If the rights agenda asked for protections, the responsibility agenda asks for obligations. Could that be why it arouses such fierce resistance? Oddly—I'd never have guessed—the responsibility agenda seems to meet stiffer resistance from much of straight America than the rights agenda ever did. At bottom, hardly anyone wants to see homosexuals harassed, but treating them as grown-ups seems more difficult to accept.

The United States has taken mighty strides to end homosexual victimhood, a fact for which I will always be grateful. What remains is to close the gap between victimhood and adulthood.

———

Now for a section which may seem digressive or unnecessary. Alas, it is neither. If there is one portion of this book I wish I didn't have to write, it is this one. But it turns out I not only need to say this but need to say it again and again:

The welfare of homosexuals counts, too.

Rick Santorum, a Republican senator from Pennsylvania, said in 2003 that marriage was fundamentally about procreation, not love. Fair enough. But when he was then asked whether he would support civil unions or other alternatives to marriage for same-sex couples, he demurred: "I'm not that familiar with civil-union laws."

"Huh?" responded Andrew Sullivan, writing in his Web log, andrewsullivan.com. "This is a U.S. senator who has put himself into the forefront of the gay debate who doesn't even know what civil unions are. You know what? I believe him. He hasn't thought for a second about the good of homosexual citizens. . . . And in this he's not alone."

Indeed he is not. Ordinary people are increasingly sympathetic to the plight of their gay friends and neighbors who form couples and assume the burdens of next-of-kinship without getting any of the prerogatives or legal tools. Among opponents of same-sex marriage, however, and especially among intellectuals of the right, it remains commonplace to regard gay people's welfare as a matter of no consequence, or of such little consequence as to be flicked aside. Assuming that 3 to 5 percent of the population is homosexual, between 9 million and 15 million Americans are gay. If there are 12 million gay Americans, that would be more than the population of any but the seven largest states, not a trivial number. Even if the number were much smaller, each gay person is an individual seeking the good life. Not one of those lives is inconsequential. Reading much of what certain opponents of same-sex marriage have to say, however, you would never realize that gay people were part of the picture at all, except as something which marriage must be saved from. The result is single-entry moral bookkeeping: the assumption that *any* harm which same-sex marriage does to heterosexuals or to the institution of marriage or (especially) to children outweighs *every* benefit to homosexuals.

For instance, writing in August 2003 in nationalreview.com, the conservative commentator Maggie Gallagher said this: "Will same-sex marriage strengthen or weaken marriage as a social institution? If the answer is that it will weaken marriage at all, we should not do it." Many conservatives would agree, except that they would replace the word "will" in the second sentence with "might": "If it *might* weaken marriage at all, we should not do it."

I concur that it is the duty of any maker of social policy to weigh costs and benefits. I have said and will always say that if same-sex marriage would destroy the institution of marriage, it is not worth having. And yet no one can make decent social policy without considering both sides of the equation. To assume that "we" (the heterosexual majority) should deny millions of Americans any chance to marry if allowing them to marry would cause "us" any harm or inconvenience at all is to account gay welfare as essentially worthless.

The point is bigger than my particular assessment of the effects of same-sex marriage. Whatever those effects may be, it remains the case that gay lives and welfare deserve to be taken as seriously as nongay lives and welfare. A one-eyed utilitarian is a blind utilitarian. I sometimes hear gay-marriage opponents say that gay marriage might increase the divorce rate or reduce respect for marriage or what have you, so we shouldn't allow it. Well, let us reflect a moment. Something like a dozen million Americans cannot marry at all. They are cut off altogether from life's most sustaining institution. The question is not whether gay marriage would raise the divorce rate or cause some other harm, but whether the harm would be of large enough magnitude to outweigh, morally and practically, the good that matrimony might bring to those millions of gay lives. I am not saying, now, that I know how the equation comes out. I am just saying that there are real people, including children (gay children and children in gay-couple households), on both sides of the equal sign.

I said earlier that possibly the cruelest element of the Long Dark Age was its failure (or refusal) to treat homosexuals with any consistency or coherence. The agenda was merely to slam any door that a homosexual was found standing in front of. Church teachings condemned adultery and fornication no less than homosexuality, but no one let that get in the way of treating homosexuality as the much more serious offense. Pastors were supposed to minister compassionately to their flock, including the sinful, since all were fallen and all could be forgiven; but for gays there was only fire and brimstone. Celibacy was an approved or at least allowed path for the homosexual in theory, but in practice even the celibate homosexual was still just a pathetic queer. One of the great iniquities of the Long Dark Age was its inculcation of an extreme moral laziness where homosexuality was concerned. People got into the habit of feeling entitled not to think about homosexuality. There was no obligation to be consistent, or to apply to homosexuals the standards which heterosexuals applied to themselves. To no small extent, that laziness persists, another cold touch of the Long Dark Age's dying hand.

I believe it is the positive duty of all caring and thoughtful citizens to struggle against moral laziness. If they do not, they do an injustice not only to gay people but also to themselves. So, getting back to the matter at issue: I think it's a safe bet that marriage and the prospect of marriage would improve gay people's health and happiness and general welfare much as it has improved straight people's; I believe it will ennoble and dignify gay love and sex as it has done straight love and sex; I believe it will close the book on the culture of libertinism and liberation and replace it with a social compact forged of responsibility. In all these respects— physical, spiritual, cultural—gay lives will be improved, at least somewhat but probably immensely. You may think I'm wrong about this or that improvement, or all of them. Say you don't believe me, fine. But please, don't say you don't care, don't know, or haven't given it much thought. Please don't say it doesn't matter. Whatever you propose doing to or for those 9 million or 12 million or 15 million gay Americans, imagine how you would react if someone proposed doing those same things to or for every one of the 12 million people who live in Illinois, or the 11 million who live in Ohio. If you insist on denying perhaps 12 million American homosexuals any hope of marrying, require yourself to consider how you would feel about denying marriage to 12 million heterosexuals. Nothing less is worthy of them or of you.

4

How Straights Will Benefit

All tragedies are finished by a death," Lord Byron writes in *Don Juan*, "All comedies are ended by a marriage." ("The future states of both," he adds wryly, "are left to faith.") From Shakespeare's day to our own, it has been a given that a wedding is a grand and happy event, a cause for rejoicing, not just for the bride and groom and their immediate families but for the whole town (and, for Shakespeare, the audience). As Byron's dry aside reminds us, marriages do not necessarily work out. Some are a triumph of hope over wisdom. And yet we rejoice nonetheless. It seems obvious, and indeed it is obvious, that, other things being equal, the union of a pair in matrimony is good news.

Obvious, at least, if the pair consists of a man and a woman. What if Bill and Bob got married? Mary and Monica? Should the community rejoice? Should it panic? Should it care?

That gay lives might improve with legal marriage seems clear enough, but that, too often, is where the plus-side accounting ends (if it happens at all). The potential costs of same-sex marriage are hashed out endlessly, sometimes in apocalyptic terms. Marriage will be wrecked, children will be devastated, polygamy will prevail across the land, and so on. Even many gay advocates of same-sex marriage tend sometimes to view the issue as purely one of gay civil rights or equality, overlooking or underappreciating the benefits to society as a whole. In this chapter and the next, I propose to redress the imbalance, at least partially. Where the nongay world is concerned, allowing gay couples to seal their bonds in law is not just a lesser of evils: it is a positive good.

———————

In his book *The Moral Sense,* James Q. Wilson observes, "A family is not an association of independent people; it is a human commitment designed to make possible the rearing of moral and healthy children. Governments care—or ought to care—about families for this reason, and scarcely for any other." Wilson here speaks of "family" rather than "marriage" as such, but I think one can read him as speaking of marriage without doing an injustice to his meaning. The resulting proposition—governments should care about marriage because of children, and scarcely for any other reason—will strike some readers as reasonable. They will conclude that governments and, by implication, societies have no compelling interest in same-sex marriage. If gay people want to cohabit, hold a ceremony, and act like a married couple, well and good. If they prefer to lead a life of solitude or celibacy, okay. If they prefer promiscuity or dissipation, that is not desirable, but it is their business.

For many years, in the United States, such was the prevalent attitude. One group of people wanted to persecute homosexuals and viewed them as a threat to the social order. A larger group, however, preferred to leave them alone and, ideally, out of sight. Society had nothing to gain by legitimizing gay relationships, and it had nothing to lose by ignoring them. Homosexuality, then, was best left as a personal and private matter. Sometimes same-sex couples (especially lesbians) would live together for years, go everywhere together, do everything together, and yet somehow their acquaintances and neighbors managed to pretend to see nothing but "inseparable friends." Isn't friendship a lovely thing?

Today, I think, someone like Wilson (I haven't asked the actual Wilson) would probably be more than willing to acknowledge a gay couple for who they are and to have the couple over for dinner. In the view of many people, the culture should accept the fact of same-sex coupledom, if only because, in today's out-and-proud world, the old pretenses have become absurd. But formal government recognition, they feel, crosses a new line and is neither necessary nor wise. No one would even be talking about it if not for the determined activism of the gay lobby. So some people maintain.

Is it true that society has no stake in same-sex marriage? I don't see how it could be.

To begin with, nowadays many gay households contain children, whether by adoption, insemination, or a previous marriage. Of the 594,000 same-sex couples counted by the Census Bureau in its 2000 survey of American households, 28 percent—just over a third of lesbian couples and just over a fifth of male couples— had children. (For married couples, the comparable figure was 46 percent.) The census doesn't say how many children lived in these households, but one or two kids per couple would translate into at least 166,000 children and possibly well over 300,000. Because gay households are rare and reticent, many demographers assume that the census figures are probably an undercount: a minimum. Other estimates put the number of gay-couple households with children at up to 2 million, and the number of children in such households at up to 3 million. Personally, I think the answer is somewhere in between, but closer to the census findings—still a large enough number to mean that, even if society cares about marriage only for the sake of children, it ought to care about the many thousands of children in gay households.

If you were the child of a same-sex couple, would you feel more secure with legally married parents, or less secure? Probably the former. If, at your tender age, you read through the social-science literature, you would certainly prefer married parents. Everything we know about children suggests they do best in stable homes, and everything we know about homes suggests that marriage makes them more stable.

You might protest that a married gay couple, particularly if male, will not be as stable as a married straight couple and so won't be as good for children. Because we have no experience with married gay couples, we have no way to know if this is true. It may or may not be. Either way, however, same-sex couples with children do not have the option of becoming opposite-sex couples with children. Moreover, forbidding gay people to raise children is neither humane nor practical (especially since many gay couples are raising one partner's *natural* children). Given the reality of children in gay households, and given the many ways in which marriage supports and sustains unions, the relevant point is that children will be more secure and happy with married gay couples than with unmarried gay couples.

If, therefore, the presence of children is what makes a relationship matter in the eyes of society, then same-sex relationships can certainly pass the test; and if the welfare of children in those relationships matters, then marriage seems the best bet. Still, we need to consider the welfare of that large majority of children in nongay households; the welfare of the many may outweigh the welfare of the few. Whether same-sex marriage will harm opposite-sex marriage is a question I'll come to later on in the book. For now, I turn to other, larger social purposes which same-sex marriage might serve.

————

Should society care if childless people get married? Should governments care? According to Wilson, no; or in any event they should not care very much. Many people today agree—or think they agree. For instance, some argue that getting divorced should be easier for people without minor children. Isn't it their own business? But folk wisdom and wise people like Shakespeare have always known better. Society's stake in marriage may begin with children, but it hardly ends there.

An aging widow takes a second husband. She is long past child-bearing age. Her children are grown and have kids of their own. But her family and friends are not dismissive or nonchalant. Unless the new husband is a scoundrel, they are happy and relieved. The wedding is an occasion for joy—more modest than many a first wedding, perhaps, but possibly more touching, too. The community receives the new couple with warm blessings. Why? No one wants to live in dotage alone, to die alone, to depend on children or, God forbid, on strangers. No one wants to be the child or stranger who is depended upon. Children or no, a marriage means one less person living on the frontier of vulnerability.

The town delinquent takes a wife. For the last few years, since he dropped out of school, he has been getting high and drunk, starting fights, having trouble holding jobs, running arrears on his rent, flitting between girlfriends, and shuttling in and out of court for minor offenses which threaten someday to become major crimes. He is not prime marriage material. One almost hopes he does not have children, at least not for a while. Yet the town breathes a sigh of relief at the news of his wedding. Why? A few farsighted people may be thinking, "When he has children, they'll be legitimate." But most people just think: "Thank goodness. Maybe he's settling down."

In both cases, the conventional wisdom is right. We all know in our gut that children are far from the only reason to care about marriage, important as children are. In chapter 1, I argued that marriage serves three essential social needs: providing a healthy environment for children (one's own and other people's), helping the young (especially men) settle down and make a home, and providing as many people as possible with caregivers. The first rationale applies only to a minority of homosexuals, namely those who are raising kids. The latter two rationales, though, apply at least as strongly to gays as to straights. Marriage will help gay people settle down, and it will help provide them with care and comfort in their hour of need—and so society will have reason to feel relieved and happy when gay couples take the vows.

Some people argue that women and children, more than just the fact of marriage, socialize and settle men. That may be true, up to a point. But that hardly means that the settling effect of marriage on gay men would be negligible. To the contrary, being tied into a committed relationship plainly helps stabilize gay men. Even without marriage, coupled gay men have steady sex partners and relationships which they value, and those things act as anchors. In American gay-male life, it's a cliché that men in relationships vanish from the clubs and the parties. "Haven't seen you out in ages," people say. "You must have found someone." Because of the realities of stitching two lives together, couples simply do not have as much time or energy for getting around, or as much desire to do so. I may have met a few gay men who prefer constant impersonal sex to a steady partner and a warm bed, but if so, I can't remember any of them. I do know some gay men—mostly of the 1960s generation—who celebrate the sexual and social libertinism of the decade before AIDS, but many of those men are now in relationships themselves. If you ask yourself whether a man in a relationship will be more wanton or less wanton than a man on his own, the answer will seem pretty obvious. Relationships are stabilizing.

And marriage stabilizes relationships. Add it to the mix, and you get the binding power of legal entitlements and entanglements, of caterers and in-laws, of the publicly acknowledged fact that the two partners are a couple. Even without kids or women, abandoning a marriage is much harder than abandoning a relationship. Gay divorce will look very much like childless straight divorce: complicated, wrenching, and a real deterrent to breaking up. (Which is one reason some gay activists of the "party on!" school are ambivalent about marriage.)

Controversy swirls around the question of the extent to which gay-male married couples will act like opposite-sex couples. It is a question I'll come back to in chapter 8, but there, as here, the only honest answer is that we don't know, because there are no gay-male married couples. It seems beyond dispute, however, that marriage will make male-male couples more settled and durable than will nonmarriage. (No one bothers to dispute that lesbian couples can and do bond durably.) The only question is: Somewhat more settled and durable, or a lot more settled and durable? As social scientists say, we may not know the magnitude of the change, but we know that the direction is positive.

Over time, as a new generation of gay children and nongay parents learn to expect and accept marriage, the cultural residue of the Long Dark Age will wash away. It is not just that today's homosexuals will become more relationship-oriented; it is that homosexual culture will become more relationship-oriented. That, too, will militate for domesticity among gay people.

Domesticity may be less of an issue for older people, but caregiving is always an issue. One of the first things many people worry about when coming to terms with their homosexuality is: Who will take care of me when I'm old? When I'm sick?

If it is true that marriage creates kin, then surely society's interest in kin creation is strongest of all for people who are less likely to have children of their own to rely on in old age and who may be rejected or even evicted—it is still not all that uncommon—by their own parents in youth. If the AIDS crisis showed anything, it was that homosexuals can and will take care of each other, sometimes with breathtaking devotion—and that no institution or government program can begin to match the love of a devoted partner.

———

It may seem a bit odd to mention the benefits of domesticity and caregiving here, under the heading of benefits for straights, rather than benefits for gays. Obviously, it is very good for homosexuals to have the security of a home and a partner. It is good for men and good for women and good for the horny young and good for the infirm old and good, period. But what may not be obvious is the stake straight society has in helping homosexuals establish settled lives. One way to see that stake is to reflect on the AIDS crisis and its enormous social cost (to say nothing of the horrific cost in gay lives). A culture of marriage might not have stopped the virus altogether, but it certainly would have slowed the virus down, and saved who knows how many lives and who knows how much money and agony. A sexual underworld is inevitable in every society, but in a marriageless society its extent is greater and its allure stronger. And, of course, its cost is higher. Syphilis, gonorrhea, and all the rest have haunted sexual underworlds since long before AIDS appeared. Beyond disease, there is a moral cost. In the context of heterosexual life, conservatives take for granted that a culture in which marriage is the norm is a healthier culture for children. It has always struck me as peculiar that so many conservatives have denounced the "homosexual lifestyle"— meaning, to a large extent, the gay sexual underworld—while fighting tooth and nail against letting gays participate in the institution which would do the most to change that lifestyle. And this, purportedly, in the name of protecting children!

What children, all children, need is protection from the bleak allure of a culture without commitment and a future without marriage. They need to grow up taking for granted that love, sex, and marriage go together—for everybody. They need to live among friends and neighbors, including gay friends and neighbors, who are married, not shacked up. No matter how you look at things, it is hard to see how a marriageless homosexual culture sends a good message for children or improves their social environment.

Some parents have gay children. That probably isn't their first choice. (Our genes want grandchildren.) Even if they understand and accept the phenomenon of homosexuality, their first thought is likely to be: "What sort of future awaits my child? How hard will his life be? What about the discrimination? What about the loneliness?" Their child may have come out to them as a teenager or a young adult. Every parent knows all too well how hard it is to get through that stage of life without making serious mistakes. Most parents would greet the prospect that their gay son or daughter could look forward to marriage with deep relief. The availability of marriage would give their child a path through the jungle. I doubt any parent would say, on learning a child is gay, "Well, thank goodness he can't marry."

The rest of us are parents of gay children, only a few steps removed. We live next door or down the block. We know instinctively that the neighborhood will be more solid if a large share of its residents are married couples. A moment's reflection suggests that the neighborhood will likewise be more solid if a large share of its homosexual residents are married couples, for all the same reasons. To say a neighborhood would be better off with fewer married gay couples and more gay singles or "domestic partners" seems perverse. Or suppose your children have a gay aunt or uncle. Suppose the neighbors' children have a gay aunt or uncle. What example would you like Uncle Jack or Aunt Janet to set?

———

As you may have noticed, all these arguments I'm making are variations on a theme. For eons, human communities have favored more marriage over less. They have believed that marriage is a powerful stabilizing force: that it disciplines and channels crazy-making love and troublemaking libido; that stability and discipline are socially beneficial, even precious. Communities everywhere believe this, and everywhere they have been right. Their belief is a deeply conservative one, based on the age-old wisdom that love and sex and marriage go together and are severed at society's peril. The question, then, boils down to this: Why should homosexuals be the one exception? Why, in fact, should the precise opposite of history's tried-and-true wisdom apply to them?

A few answers are possible. One is that homosexuality is bad and legitimizing homosexuality will produce more of it. That view misunderstands homosexuality. A small fraction of the population is homosexual and cannot reasonably do anything about it and will fall in love and form couples and do so openly. The question is whether society is better off with homosexuals doing those things inside or outside the confines of marriage. What does society gain by excluding them?

A second answer is that marriage will not have the same effects on gays as on straights. The most common version of this argument—namely, that gay men will get married but not act married—I take up in chapter 8. Here let me just say again that it is very hard to see how legal marriage could make gay relationships *less* successful or enduring. The question is only how much it would help.

A third answer is that homosexuals will simply not get married. They will view matrimony as a minority taste, and so society won't get much out of the deal. After all, only a minority of gay people in Vermont seem to be signing up for civil unions.

I confess this last possibility worries me. If it is good for society to have people durably attached, then it is not enough just to make marriage available. Marriage should also be *expected*. That is as true for gays as for straights. So, if homosexuals are justified in expecting access to marriage, society is equally justified in expecting them to use it. If marriage is to work, it cannot be merely a "lifestyle option." It must be privileged. That is, it must be understood to be better than other ways of living. Not mandatory, not good where everything else is bad, but better: a general norm, rather than a personal taste. Gay neglect of marriage would not greatly erode the bonding power of heterosexual marriage; homosexuals are, after all, only a small fraction of the population. But it would certainly not help. In any case, the benefits to gay people and to society obviously materialize only to the extent that gay people actually get married. Heterosexual society would rightly feel betrayed if, after legalization, homosexuals treated marriage as a minority taste rather than as a core institution of life.

No one knows how homosexuals will respond to legal marriage. My guess is that only a minority will marry at the beginning, after legalization. But then? Here it becomes important to say a word about the element of time.

––––––

Russians and East Europeans suffered under Communist rule for seventy years. Even before Communism they had not known freedom, and then Communism plunged them into a world of utter repression. Told that they could not do what they must do and that they must do what they could not do, people and societies bent to the point of dysfunction. Individuals learned to mistrust one another, to game the system, to regard personal initiative as a fool's errand. Logic itself, the daily logic of living, became warped. "The Soviet system is basically senseless," wrote the Russian dissident Andrei Amalrik. "Like a paranoiac, it *behaves* logically; but since its premises are senseless, the same is true of the results."

Then one day it ended. Down came the wall, down came the regime. Many Westerners expected a rapid flowering of democracy and capitalism in the former Soviet Union and its satellites. Just watch as the miracle of capitalism unfolds! Instead, we saw only halting progress. After a while, disappointment set in. But the disappointment was as unrealistic as the earlier optimism. Adjusting a culture to the twin shocks of freedom and responsibility takes time, probably a few generations. People need to relearn who they are. They need to build trust and a new social compact. Nowadays, most Western observers have come to see the transition out of Communism as a work in progress. Yes, it could be going faster, and in some places it isn't really going at all. But the wonder is that it is going so well.

Homosexuals have suffered under a Long Dark Age of not seventy years but seven hundred or more. Until as recently as the 1960s, there was no place, not anywhere, where gay people were at liberty to be themselves. As with the coming of capitalism to the Soviet empire, so with the coming of marriage to gay culture. Freedom and responsibility take time to learn.

The wonder is not how slowly gay culture is maturing but how quickly. Recently I had coffee with my friend Dale, who, at forty-one, was in a relationship with a man of twenty-four. We had a conversation which is becoming something of a staple among gay men in their forties. Dale marveled at how naturally his partner, Bill, had settled into the relationship. Bill just seemed to assume that domesticity was his birthright. I asked if faithfulness wasn't a problem for a twenty-four-year-old man with a forty-one-year-old partner. No, Dale replied. At the ripe age of twenty-four, Bill had already had his fill of one-night stands. Then we indulged in the obligatory moment of wistful head shaking. Gay men our age sound like geezers: "Why, these young people today—they have no idea how lucky they are!" Many a gay man of twenty-four thinks nothing, now, of leaving behind the sexual adolescence that his elders spent much of their lives floundering in.

Gay culture is changing, in large part because society has come to tolerate and, increasingly, even accept same-sex relationships. But the event that signaled the start of gay liberation, the Stonewall riot, occurred as recently as 1969, and the biggest change of all, the entitlement of gay couples to marriage, has yet to be introduced. If and when gay marriage is introduced, expect progress, not miracles. Expect a few decades between the legalization of same-sex marriage and its full integration into gay lives and culture.

Remember, not one same-sex couple has ever married, expected to marry, or even hoped to marry. Having built their relationships and lives outside marriage, often in the face not only of legal indifference but of social hostility, many gay adults will see marriage as an optional but hardly necessary government imprimatur. Others will be ideologically opposed. Marriage? That's for straights! Still others, viewing marriage as a way to get health insurance, will marry for the benefits, as heterosexuals sometimes marry for money. Yet others will hesitate to marry because parents or close family don't know they are gay or want to keep pretending not to know. At first, in other words, many gays will not marry, and some will marry for the wrong reasons or too casually. And, of course, some will head straight to the courthouse and do matrimony proud.

How the numbers will shake out is impossible to say. The question, though, is not primarily one of speed but of direction. Marriage, with the prestige and prerogatives and security and expectations it brings, has a way of putting down roots even in rocky soil. My guess is that there is a tipping point out there somewhere. As personal and legal and communal expectations reinforce each other—as gay people get used to asking themselves, "Could this relationship lead to marriage?"—a time will come when same-sex marriage crosses from new and exotic to established and expected. Then the Long Dark Age will really be over.

Is it possible that, even several decades after legalization, gay marriage will turn out to be a minority choice, an adornment rather than an institution? Yes. Anything is possible. But I would bet on marriage as the choice of the masses, just as I would bet on democracy and capitalism, because marriage, like democracy and capitalism, meets the personal and social needs of human beings as nothing else can.

To the skeptics I would say: I can't prove you wrong. But do you really want to bet *against* marriage? Do you want to put your money on quasi-marriage or semimarriage or nonmarriage? That would not be a particularly conservative bet. Indeed, it would be a radical one.

5

How Marriage Will Benefit

And now, as they say, for the hard part.

To persuade people that the institution of marriage might improve the lives of gay people is not difficult. To persuade them that society has a stake in improving the lives of gay people is harder, but still doable. But to persuade people that radically redefining marriage (as they would say) might be good for the institution itself, strengthening it rather than undermining it, is a real challenge.

Nonetheless, a key premise of this book is that legalizing same-sex marriage would indeed strengthen the meaning and mission and message of marriage, both in comparison with the alternatives and in its own right. I firmly believe this to be true. I believe that preserving the ban on same-sex marriage will in fact weaken marriage, a little at first but then more over time, by blurring its boundaries and eroding its prestige. In other words, friends of marriage today do not have a choice between radically redefining marriage and leaving marriage alone. They must choose between maintaining marriage's exclusivity and maintaining its special status.

This is an entirely new situation. In the past, everyone could safely assume that marriage's exclusivity and prestige went together.

Indeed, the idea of opening marriage to "sodomites" seemed laugh-able, disgusting, or both. To propose letting a man "marry" a man was like proposing to let a man "marry" a Volkswagen.

Many people, of course, make exactly that point today. Same-sex marriage, they say, would by definition not be marriage at all. It would empty marriage of its meaning, its legitimacy, its status. For that reason, many opponents refer not to gay marriage but to gay "marriage," with the quotation marks. But people who think mar-riage's meaning and specialness depend on the exclusion of same-sex couples have got it backward. The reason is a bend in the river of history: a fundamental change in society's view of human sexual-ity—a change which cannot be undone, should not be undone, and must be reckoned with whether one approves of it or not. It can be summarized in two words: homosexuals exist. That changes everything, not least how marriage is best preserved and protected.

If everyone is heterosexual, then same-sex relations are at best a crass frolic, like sodomy at sea, and at worst an act of domination or abuse, like prison sex or a fraternity hazing. In an all-heterosex-ual world, if some people are determined to have same-sex rela-tions despite all the discouragements and punishments society can mete out, they must have an inner moral or mental sickness, which warps the true heterosexual self and ought not to be indulged. Obviously, marriage should not accommodate the bizarre tastes of the "practicing homosexual." Rather, the homosexual—who is in fact a disturbed heterosexual—should change his prac-tices and accommodate himself to marriage.

Only in the last couple of generations has the everyone-is-heterosexual model collapsed. If homosexuality were merely a behavior indulged in by heterosexuals, after all, centuries of the fiercest repression should have stamped it out; yet it persisted. If, on the other hand, homosexual behavior presented an irresistible temptation to heterosexuals, whole societies should have turned gay; but they never did. In his book *Sex and Reason* (1992), the jurist Richard A. Posner summed up the facts concisely:

> Homosexual preference, especially male homosexual prefer-
> ence, appears to be widespread; perhaps to be innate (the
> implication of the studies of identical twins and of the recent
> brain studies); to exist in most, perhaps all, societies, whether
> they are tolerant of homosexuality or repressive of it; to be
> almost completely—perhaps completely—resistant to treat-
> ment; and to be no more common in tolerant than in repres-
> sive societies. . . . Given the personal and social disadvantages
> to which homosexuality subjects a person in our society, the
> idea that millions of young men and women have chosen it or
> will choose it in the same fashion in which they might choose a
> career or a place to live or a political party or even a religious
> faith seems preposterous.

Today not even the Vatican denies that some people (not many) are so constituted as to be homosexual, even if acting on their constitution remains a sin. With the exception of a small "ex-gay" movement (whose followers have a way of turning out not to be so "ex"), most people have given up on the notion that homosexuals would be heterosexual if they tried a little harder, or that heterosexuals would be homosexual if the law didn't stop them. Many people continue to distinguish between gay people and gay sex ("love the sinner, hate the sin"). Many regard same-sex relationships as inferior if not wicked. And so the day when the public uniformly views homosexuality as nothing more than the sexual equivalent of left-handedness has yet to dawn. Still: a large *and growing* number of Americans accept that a small and basically stable share of the population cannot flourish within opposite-sex relationships. They have accepted that homosexual-ity exists.

I emphasize the words "and growing" because it seems clear that the river has bent for good. As time goes on, gay individuals will only continue to live more openly, gay couples will only continue to grow more visible, and the idea that homosexuality is a disease or a miserable perversion will only become less consistent with evident facts. Now marriage faces an entirely new question: not "Should marriage be defined in such a way as to discourage aberrant sexual behavior?" but "Should marriage be defined in such a way as to exclude a class of people altogether?"

In other words, will marriage be defined by what it expects or by whom it excludes? That is the issue which marriage must resolve. Our ancestors never had to confront this choice, but we do.

———

I often hear people say that the reason gays want to be able to marry is to normalize homosexuality. There are actually quite a few reasons gays want marriage, but change "the reason" in the previous sentence to "a reason" and the statement is hard to quibble with. Homosexuals are indeed tired of being seen as "perverts" or "deviants" or "queers"—who wouldn't be?—and legalizing same-sex marriage would signal that the law, for its part, recognizes that some people happen to be gay. But what is more important about legalizing same-sex matrimony is that it would normalize *marriage*. Or, if you prefer, it would renormalize marriage. It would shore up marriage's unique but eroding status as the preferred structure for two people who want to build a life together.

In chapter 2, I mentioned that the surest way to break marriage's status as the norm is to surround it with competitors which offer most of the benefits but few of the burdens, as is happening with domestic-partner programs intended for gay couples but extended to straight couples as well. The only way to arrest this slide is to level the playing field. Go back to Rule 1. In fact, reinforce it. "If you want the benefits of marriage, *get married*—no exclusions, no exceptions, no excuses." Adopt same-sex marriage, and the alternatives-to-marriage movement loses its main impetus overnight. Straight activists who want nonmarital options would no longer be

able to piggyback on the movement to grant gay couples some form
of legal recognition. They would have to live or die on the strength
of the proposition that *heterosexuals* need alternatives to marriage.
That does not mean the alternatives-to-marriage movement would
pack its bags and move to Argentina. But the movement's legitimacy and appeal would be immensely diminished.

The long-term benefit to marriage would not be small. The
potential market for same-sex marriages is probably no more than
5 percent of the population; but the potential market for partner
programs encompasses the whole population. Although no one
can be sure, eventually enough employers and government jurisdictions might adopt straight-inclusive domestic-partner programs
to make legal partnership widely competitive with marriage. The
preference of parents and religious institutions for no-kidding,
old-fashioned, lace-gown marriages might slow down the assimi-
lation of marriage-lite, but, in time, religious leaders and parents
would accept what growing numbers of heterosexual couples
were doing. It is even possible (although I wouldn't give odds)
that, a generation from now, legal marriage might seem not so
much prestigious as anachronistic.

So the first way same-sex marriage can normalize marriage is by
denormalizing the alternatives. I have yet to see any prominent—
or, come to think of it, nonprominent—gay-marriage opponent
say one word about the problem of proliferating competition. To
me, ignoring the consequences of the alternatives seems irresponsible. It won't do to say, "Just stop gay marriage and worry
about the rest later." Later is already now.

———

But now on to a second point. Legally recognized domestic-
partner and civil-union programs are not the only competitors to
marriage. Another is cohabitation. And it is a biggie.

According to the 2000 census, during the 1990s the number
of unmarried-partner households in the United States increased

by 72 percent. Cohabitation has been rising for decades, but starting from a small base. Now the numbers (more than 5 million cohabiting couples, the vast majority of them heterosexual) are beginning to look impressive. Marriage, meanwhile, is headed in the other direction. The marriage rate (defined as the annual number of weddings per thousand single women age fifteen or older) fell by 40 percent from 1970 to 2000. Many factors have been at work—people are marrying later, for example—but it seems clear that the rise in cohabitation is among them. People are simply more willing to live together without tying the knot.

Whether this development is a bad thing is a contentious question, but it is probably not a good thing. Marriages tend to be more durable and healthy than cohabitations, even after one accounts (as best one can) for differences in the relevant populations. For all the reasons I discussed in earlier chapters, marriage itself brings something important to the table. Add the fact that a growing share of cohabiting households—now more than a third—contain children, and it is hard to be enthusiastic about the trend.

Cohabitation used to be stigmatized. "Living in sin," it was called. Today more than a few people view it as a different-but-equal alternative to wedlock. "Why do I need a piece of paper?" is something most of us have heard somebody ask. Although the drift toward cohabitation would no doubt have happened anyway, it seems likely that the growing visibility and acceptance of same-sex couples—virtually all of them cohabitants in the eyes of the law—sped up the change. As one gay activist told the *Los Angeles Times*, "Just the term 'unmarried partner' gave it a dignity and social category."

So, conservatives say, it's true! Homosexuals undermine marriage! The culprit, however, is not the presence of same-sex couples; it is the absence of same-sex marriage.

Like other mass civic institutions, from voting to the draft to elementary education, marriage draws crucial strength from its universality. Rule 1: "If you want the benefits of marriage, *get married.*" Essential corollary to Rule 1: "And that means you!" Obviously, if the law says that not everybody can marry, the law says that not everybody should marry. The more exceptions, carve-outs, and special cases, the harder it is to project a clear, unequivocal message that marriage (or voting or military service or schooling or what have you) is for everybody, and that means you. Instead the message becomes, "Well, marriage is for *most* people. Cohabitation is for homosexuals."

You might object that many mass civic institutions disqualify some people. The military disqualifies the infirm (and, come to think of it, open homosexuals). Felons often lose the right to vote, even after serving their sentences (a dumb rule, in my opinion). I can't think of any exception to the rule that everyone has to go to school up to a certain age, but there may be one. Conservatives argue that being a man and a man or a woman and a woman disqualifies a couple from marrying.

What they miss is that a growing number of homosexuals are acting married and being regarded by their heterosexual peers as married in all but law. The risk is that the culture and the law will part ways as gay people set up what amount to common-law marriages, becoming spouses unofficially but cohabitants in the eyes of the law. The very distinction between marriage and cohabitation blurs as couples' behavior, rather than their legal status, comes to be accepted as the dividing line. Just look outside or turn on the TV to see examples of a whole group of relatively successful and attractive Americans among whom love and romance and sex and commitment flourish entirely outside marriage. Conservatives who believe that the denial of marriage will prolong the stigmatization of homosexuals may be 'in for an unpleasant surprise. The growing visibility of unmarried gay couples may legitimize cohabitation instead. The marriage ban turns gays into walking billboards for the irrelevance of marriage.

The emergence into the open of same-sex relationships is an irreversible fact. So is the increasing acknowledgment that homosexuals exist. Many people, even many conservatives, know and accept gay couples as friends and neighbors. As minorities go, gays are fairly influential, culturally speaking. Homosexuals are here, we're queer, and nowadays we're kind of cool. Think about *Will and Grace, Queer Eye for the Straight Guy,* and that gay guy who won *Survivor.* This isn't to say that Americans want to be gay, that gays have an easy time in school, or that gays in Hollywood lead the culture around by the nose. The point is that offering every homosexual couple as a potential example of successful life outside of wedlock is not a good idea in a country where plenty of people are already deciding that marriage is an unnecessary hassle. Opponents of same-sex marriage who worry that gays would set a bad example by marrying ought to be more worried about the example gays are already setting by *not* marrying.

In getting this backward, anti-gay-marriage conservatives make a mistake which is both ironic and sad. At a time when marriage needs all the support and participation it can get, homosexuals are pleading to move beyond cohabitation. They want the licenses, the vows, the rings, the honeymoons, the anniversaries, the in-laws, the benefits, and, yes, the responsibilities and the routines. Same-sex marriage offers the opportunity for a dramatic public affirmation that marriage is for everybody and that nothing else is as good. And who is telling gays to just shack up instead? The self-styled friends of matrimony.

The issues here are fundamental. Conservatives who oppose same-sex marriage want to be able to say, as conservatives have rightly said for many generations, "Sex, love, and marriage go together." But they also want to say, "Same-sex couples can't get married." Until society recognized the existence of homosexuals, conservatives could maintain both propositions; but now they must choose. They can defend marriage's normality or its exclusivity, but not both.

Either choice bears its share of risk. I believe that the norm of sex-love-marriage is the one to go with, because the norm of opposite-sex-only is less important and less fair and is crumbling anyway as the culture adjusts to the reality of same-sex unions. The fundamental conflict today, if you care about marriage, is not between same-sex marriage and traditional marriage; it is between marriage and nonmarriage. We have reached the proverbial cross-roads, but the task is not to choose one of two roads; it is to choose between one road and all roads. We can go together down the road of marriage for everyone, or we can scatter among a multitude of paths, of which marriage is but one.

———

Same-sex marriage, then, clarifies and reinforces the key message to people who are embarking on coupledom: marriage is for everybody, marriage is unique—no exceptions, exclusions, or excuses. In doing so, gay matrimony bolsters marriage's status as the gold standard for committed relationships, at a time when marriage's competitors are gaining ground. And in so doing it also preserves and strengthens marriage's legitimacy and sustainability as a social and legal institution. It stabilizes marriage for the long haul.

What, am I crazy? Isn't the whole problem that letting men marry men (or dogs or Volkswagens) will undermine the legitimacy of marriage by declaring matrimony to be something it plainly isn't? People say this all the time, and they have a point. If the law recognized same-sex marriages while communities and churches and many ordinary people renounced them, that could be a mess.

A fair objection, and one I take up at length in chapter 10. For now, suffice to say that keeping legal marriage in line with social marriage is indeed important—but if marriage law can get too far ahead of what the culture views as matrimony, it can also get too far behind. If the too precipitous adoption of same-sex marriage risks undercutting the institution's legitimacy in the public's eyes, the dogmatic insistence on a same-sex-marriage ban presents the same problem—only squared. As it is currently structured, legal marriage is increasingly at odds with modern liberalism's core concept: the principle of equality before the law. The misalignment between principle and practice is not going away and is not sustainable, and if same-sex-marriage opponents refuse to acknowledge and fix it, they are playing with fire. To see why, we need to dig all the way to the fundamental premise that makes a society like America cohere: the liberal concept of justice.

"All men are created equal," says the Declaration of Independence, in words every schoolchild can (I hope) recite. "They are endowed by their Creator with certain unalienable rights, [and] among these are life, liberty, and the pursuit of happiness." For homosexuals no less than heterosexuals, home and family and security and status are at the heart of the pursuit of happiness. Marriage is an irreplaceable ingredient in the quest for home and family and security and status; and so, if the Declaration's words mean anything, they suggest that to deprive millions of Americans of any hope of an emotionally satisfying relationship—marriage—is unjust (and I would add cruel) unless doing so is absolutely necessary.

"Ah, but it is necessary, that is the whole point," you might say. "The law is not 'depriving' same-sex couples of the right to marry, because, by definition, same-sex couples can't *be* married. Same-sex marriage would be a contradiction in terms, and so rejecting it can hardly be unjust. Indeed, allowing it would be a parody of justice, like putting a cat on a jury."

At one level, I can't really argue with someone who takes that position. In effect, he is saying that marriage is defined not by the vows (homosexuals can take them) or by devotion and fidelity (homosexuals are capable of both) or even by children (many heterosexuals cannot or do not have them, and some homosexuals do), but by its exclusion of homosexuals. Marriage is a club defined simply by who cannot join; its very essence is discrimination against same-sex applicants. This, I submit, is a dangerous way to define marriage, because in practice it is headed for a collision with the five most important words in the American social contract: "All men are created equal."

Equal, here, does not mean *the same.* Yes, men and women are different (on average). Yes, male-female, male-male, and female-female marriages would differ (on average—although I expect the differences within the three groups would often be greater than the differences between them). *Equal* means *equal before the law.*

Equality before the law does not oblige the government to apply the law without regard to individuals' or groups' needs or circumstances. It does mean this: in a liberal democracy, "democracy" refers to government by the consent of the people, but "liberal" requires the government to *treat similarly situated people in a similar way.*

Now, the fundamental question in the gay-marriage debate is: Who is similarly situated? One school of thought, which I just alluded to, holds that same-sex couples are not at all similar to opposite-sex couples. "Of course, the law applies the same way to everyone," goes the thinking. "The rule says that everyone can marry someone of the opposite sex. Homosexuals are perfectly free to do that. The law is certainly fair, even if perhaps nature is not."

It is nature, however, which has made this view untenable. More specifically, it is the realization that homosexuals do indeed exist. Like it or not, homosexual men need the love and touch of men, and homosexual women need the love and touch of women; and until the reality of homosexuality is accepted in law, it will gnaw at marriage's legitimacy. For it is increasingly clear that homosexuals are not comparably treated by today's marriage law, at least not if you think sex, love, and marriage go together. In the United States, homosexuals cannot legally marry *anyone* they love. There is *no* heterosexual in this position. True, not all heterosexuals find someone to marry. But every heterosexual, without exception, is given the opportunity to marry for love (and for sex); and most regard the hope of a love marriage as the sine qua non of the pursuit of happiness—ahead of career, money, fame, even children. Under the law as it stands, not one homosexual can pursue this dream.

Sex, love, and marriage go together to form integrated lives and integrated unions. A marriage which cannot satisfy the heart and flesh is not a marriage which is likely to work. If I belabor the point, it is because some same-sex-marriage opponents really do say, "Look, marriage is about children, not love, and if homosexuals want to marry, let them just find someone of the opposite gender and skip the sex." Never mind the cruelty of pretending to love someone so he or she will marry you, or the crassness of forming a marriage as a kind of loveless business arrangement. Never mind the irony of hearing conservatives insist that gay men should not be allowed to marry because they will cheat on each other, only to hear them suggest in the very next breath that gay men marry women whom they will almost inevitably cheat on. (As Benjamin Franklin quipped: "Where there's marriage without love, there will be love without marriage.") The core problem here is that no one would ever dream of telling heterosexuals they could marry *only* people they did *not* love. It would be insane. Yet that is the position in which homosexuals now find themselves.

Americans' commitment to equality under the law—to liberalism—is the country's essential social contract. It is the glue that binds a diverse population into a nation. Again and again it has overmastered the insistence that this or that mass civic institution is defined by whom it excludes, rather than by what it expects. When it became obvious that blacks were not children and that women could think for themselves, the country had to make a choice: expand the franchise or see it lose its legitimacy. Marriage's position today is similar. As gay couples (and their children) weave themselves into their neighborhoods and communities, new facts are arising on the ground. To say, "Well, that may be, but marriage simply cannot accommodate those facts and still be marriage," is no answer at all. It assures that other, nonmarital arrangements will arise and gain legitimacy. Worse, nonmarriage—civil unions, domestic partnerships, cohabitation—may acquire *greater* legitimacy than marriage. After all, isn't a nondiscriminatory institution better? In my lifetime, clubs which insisted they were upholding the natural way of doing things by excluding women or Jews turned out to be consigning themselves to oblivion. The changing culture simply left them behind. In much the same way, straights-only marriage could soon have the dubious distinction of being "the *discriminatory* lifestyle choice." Cohabitation and partnership may emerge as ethically modern, while marriage becomes your father's Oldsmobile.

So that is another way in which, by hoping to use marriage to marginalize homosexuality, gay-marriage opponents risk marginalizing marriage instead. Not right away, but over time. To continue to insist that gays must never marry demeans gays, but much more worrisome is that it will demean marriage.

———

"With all due respect to proponents of same-sex marriage," writes William J. Bennett in his book *The Broken Hearth: Reversing the Collapse of the American Family* (2001), "it is also important to say publicly what most of us believe privately, namely, that marriage between a man and a woman is in every way to be preferred to the marriage of two men or two women." Here he makes a point which is, for many people, a bottom-line objection to gay marriage. If the law blesses homosexual unions, wouldn't it be saying they are the equivalent of heterosexual unions? That goes beyond toleration, which these days most Americans favor. It implies—doesn't it?—acceptance of homosexuality, which many people still object to. In fact, doesn't it go all the way to approval—which many Americans stoutly reject? And, really, isn't that what homosexuals want, with their drive for marriage: approval?

Marriage is a social institution; and, so far, I have analyzed it from that perspective. But marriage is also law. If it's true that marriage-as-law needs to stay in reasonably close step with mar-riage-as-social-institution, it is also the case that marriage-as-law must stay in reasonably close step with law-as-law. I want to make a legal point by way of reply to Bennett and others who seek to pre-vent marriage's being used as (in their view) an instrument of forced approbation. First, however, let me clear away a few smaller points.

I have to say, if the reader will permit me a moment of exasper-ation, that we homosexuals get a bit tired of being assured by het-erosexuals that their loves and lives and unions are "in every way" better than ours. For one thing, I value my love and life and union as much as Bill Bennett values his, and most gay people I know would say the same. It is particularly tiresome for two gay part-ners who have been together through thick and thin for ten or twenty years to be told that, no matter how hard they work to do right by each other and their community, their union is "in every way" inferior to that of the straight couple next door who got hitched last month and will split up as soon as the sex gets old. Dale Carpenter, a University of Minnesota law professor and same-sex-marriage advocate, puts it vividly:

> When my partner was in the hospital, near death, he was so stricken by high fever that I put my body around his to keep him warm so he could sleep. When his mother was brain-dead and they were about to cut off her life support, I pulled him from her bedside and held him and felt a pain so deep inside me it has never left. When I was out of a job, he supported me. When I felt unworthy or dumb, he made me feel like a god in his arms. If some advocates of gay marriage have little understanding or appreciation for the richness and depth of marriage, it's also true that some opponents of gay marriage have little understanding or appreciation for the richness and depth of gay life.
>
>   Instead, we get offered a cartoonish view of gay couples as hyperpromiscuous, disco-era selfish, incapable of real commit-ment, unfit to raise children. And gays get all this criticism

simply for wanting to make a civilized public commitment to each other. I wonder what they would be saying about gays if we *weren't* pressing for the right to marry.

And another thing, while I'm complaining. I don't have the choice of being heterosexual, and marrying a woman is not an option for me (at least not if the woman knows what's good for her), so what exactly is the point of saying, in effect, that it would be "in every way to be preferred" if I were straight? I certainly agree that male-female marriage is "in every way to be preferred" for heterosexuals, but surely it is also clear that same-sex marriage is preferable to nonmarriage for homosexuals—given that we do, in fact, exist.

As it happens, I experience my own homosexuality as a (mild) disability. If I could have designed myself in the womb, I would have chosen to be heterosexual, because I feel I am missing out on something special and irreplaceable by not being able to conceive and raise a child with the partner I love. On the other hand, I say the disability is mild because most people need to do without some important opportunity. Life is like that. We play the hand we're dealt.

But that leads me to the big point, the point about marriage-as-law. Look again at Bennett's statement: "With all due respect to proponents of same-sex marriage, it is also important to say publicly . . . that marriage between a man and a woman is in every way to be preferred." If by "saying publicly" he means just writing his opinion in a book, he is more than entitled. Given that he is defending the ban on same-sex marriage, however, I think what he means is that the law, and not just Bill Bennett, should affirm the superiority of heterosexual relationships. Marriage is approval. The law should withhold it.

With all due respect to opponents of same-sex marriage, discriminating in order to pin a badge of inferiority on some group or another is not a legitimate use of law. There are all sorts of ways in which individuals, religious bodies, community groups, or politicians can appropriately express their belief that gay relationships are inferior to straight ones, but creating legal infirmities is not one of them. It is not as if homosexuals have decided, against their own better judgment, to be gay. They are just doing the best they can to find love and build lives, the same as everyone else. Their loves and lives are no less worthy than heterosexual loves and lives; but suppose, for the sake of argument, that heterosexual unions are in some important sense preferable. The law's job is not to punish the disadvantaged by excluding them but to help them make the most of their lives, or at least to give them the same benefit of the doubt which is accorded everyone else.

I am not the first to make this point. In 1858, during his debates with Abraham Lincoln, Senator Stephen A. Douglas argued that it was incontrovertible that blacks were not the equals of whites and that the law should reflect the facts: "He [Lincoln] believes the Negro, by divine law, is created the equal of the white man, and that no human law can deprive him of that equality, thus secured; and he contends that the Negro ought therefore to have all the rights and privileges of citizenship on an equality with the white man. . . . Why, he would permit them to marry, would he not?"

Douglas was being cagey here. He knew that the public was readier to confer at least some legal rights upon blacks than to acknowledge that the black man was fully the equal of the white man—something which very few whites, in those days, believed. So Douglas implied that equality-in-law and equality-in-fact must go together, and that Lincoln stood for both; and if blacks were deemed equal-in-fact to whites, it was but a short slippery slope to complete legal equality for blacks, including legal marriage between the races—a horrifying prospect to many whites in that day. "If the divine law declares that the white man is the equal of

the Negro woman, that they are in perfect equality," said Douglas,
"I suppose he admits the right of the Negro woman to marry the
white man."

Lincoln was no less cagey than Douglas. He knew it was political suicide to declare the black man fully the equal of the white
man, and so, in his famous reply to Douglas, he did not declare it.
Instead he said this:

> I have said that I do not understand the Declaration [of Inde-
> pendence] to mean that all men are created equal in all
> respects. They are not our equal in color; but I suppose that it
> does mean to declare that all men are equal in some respects;
> that they are equal in their right to "life, liberty, and the pursuit
> of happiness." Certainly the Negro is not our equal in color—
> perhaps not in many other respects; still, in the right to put
> into his mouth the bread that his own hands have earned, he is
> the equal of every other man, white or black. In pointing out
> that more has been given to you, you cannot be justified in tak-
> ing away the little which has been given to him. All I ask for
> the Negro is that if you do not like him, let him alone. If God
> gave him but little, that little let him enjoy.

Lincoln, evading Douglas's trap, neither concedes nor contests
black inferiority. He sidesteps that question to make a deeper
point. *If* blacks are inferior—so what? Disadvantaging the inferior
is not a proper use of law; indeed, it flies in the face of the Declaration's promise.

Lincoln's argument was subtle, delicate—above all, counterin-
tuitive; yet history has proved it right. There may be many practical
and principled reasons to support the exclusion of homosexuals
from the institution of civil marriage, and the law's job is to do the
reasonable thing. But to whatever extent the legal exclusion's
purpose is merely to affirm the heterosexual majority's belief in
homosexual inferiority, the law is being abused. Whether to condemn, tolerate, accept, approve, or celebrate same-sex unions is

your own business and entirely your prerogative. But the law's job, at least its essential job, is to do none of those things. The law's job is to give everyone a fair and equal shake. And civil marriage is, apart from everything else, a law. Abuse it, and you will damage it. Better to say, following Lincoln: *if* homosexuals are allotted a lesser kind of love, let them make the most of it.

———

I am not suggesting that there is a constitutional right to gay marriage. I am only reminding you that the question at hand is not whether same-sex marriages should be approved of but whether they should be *legal*. The government may disapprove of many things, but it should ban them only if they harm other people, harm society, or violate somebody's rights: not simply as a gesture of contempt.

So we arrive at the crucial question. Gay marriage does not seem likely to violate anyone's rights. But would it harm other people or society? Having looked at the benefits of gay marriage, in the next four chapters I turn to what its opponents say are the prohibitive costs.

6

Married, Without Children

In July 1996, Representative Barney Frank, an openly gay
member of Congress from Massachusetts, asked a question
which proved difficult to answer. The Defense of Marriage Act
was on the floor of the House, and Frank wanted to know: How
would my marrying another man threaten your marriage? He
described asking supporters of the bill, one by one:

> How does the fact that two men live together in a loving rela-
> tionship and commit themselves in Hawaii threaten your mar-
> riage in Florida or Georgia or wherever? And the answer is
> always, well, it does not threaten my marriage, it threatens the
> institution of marriage. That, of course, baffles me some. Insti-
> tutions do not marry. They may merge, but they do not marry.
> People marry, human beings. Men and women who love each
> other marry. And no one who understands human nature
> thinks that allowing two other people who love each other
> interferes.

Where heterosexuals are concerned, we generally take for
granted that marriage is a positive-sum game, good for the marrying couple (assuming they are good for each other) and good for

everyone else. America has a problem with too few marriages, not too many. One would think that encouraging a whole new population of cohabitants to tie the knot would be a step in the right direction. Yet where homosexuals are concerned, the standard assumptions are turned on their head. Same-sex marriage is seen by many as a win-lose proposition at best; gays who want to marry should be thought of not as recruits but as attackers. Barney Frank was asking: Huh? He was not alone in suspecting that the real problem with gay marriage isn't with marriage at all, but with gays. Was prejudice masquerading as reason?

One option, of course, is just to reply, "By definition, marriage is between a man and a woman, and that's that." But that serves only to answer the question "Why shouldn't gay couples be allowed to marry?" by replying, "Because I said so." (Or "Because God said so.") To their chagrin, opponents of same-sex marriage were being told they needed to do better. Since 1996, to their credit, they have done better, and they have found a lot to say about both marriage and homosexuality. Again and again, however, they run into the same problem. Given the way marriage is socially practiced and legally structured in the United States, most theories which exclude homosexuals from marriage also exclude many heterosexuals— including many heterosexuals who are happily married. Well, there is one thing no homosexual couple can do, and that is to procreate. So gay-marriage opponents come back time and again, at the outset and then as a last resort, to the claim that marriage is inseparable from children and procreation.

There are so many formulations of the marriage-children-procreation nexus, and so many of them are so vague, that they become difficult to pin down. Some people say marriage is for children, others say it is for procreation (which is not the same thing); some argue that children are an essential reason for marriage, others that children are the only reason for marriage; some contend that marriage is good for children, others that childlessness is bad for marriage. Most often, people just mash together various and sundry of the above. Here is as good an example as any, from comments by Senator Rick Santorum in August 2003:

> I think, to most people in America, number one, it's common sense that a marriage is between a man and a woman. I mean, every civilization in the history of man has recognized a unique bond. Why? Because—principally because of children. I mean, it's—it is the reason for marriage. . . . Marriage is not about affirming somebody's love for somebody else. It's about uniting together to be open to children, to further civilization in our society.
>
> And that's unique. And that's why civilizations forever have recognized that unique role that needs to be licensed, needs to be held up as different than anything else because of its unique nurturing effect on children. And there isn't a statistic out there that doesn't show that married couples, in a healthy marriage, is the best environment in which to raise stable children and is the best thing, long term, for our society.

What to make of that? Really it is a cascading series of arguments and assumptions. The best way to proceed, probably, is to unpack the bundle of "married, without children" arguments into a series of related but distinct propositions, which together cover all the bases I can think of.

1. Marriage is uniquely good for raising children.
2. Without children, marriage isn't worth having.
3. Without *natural* children (i.e., procreation), marriage isn't worth having.
4. Without the *possibility* of natural children (i.e., openness to procreation), marriage isn't worth having.
5. Without sex of the *type* which produces children, marriage isn't worth having.

Let us delve in.

For some readers, this book so far suffers from a glaring omission. Where are the children? The majority of married couples have children at some point, and many of the ones who don't have children planned on having them when they got married, and some got married because they had children, and children are typically the central preoccupation of married couples who are raising them. How can anyone possibly write a book on marriage while leaving children mostly out of the picture?

Guilty as charged. Children are a very important part of the marriage picture, and I have given them short shrift so far. Here, then, is the place to affirm Proposition 1: *Marriage is uniquely good for raising children*. Children need stability, security, affection, socialization, resources, moral instruction. Marriage does a better job of providing those than does any other arrangement we know. For a while in the 1970s, people said that the most important thing for children was for their parents to be happy, but that appears not to be true. More important (on average—always on average) is that their parents be *together*. A single-parent home is (on average) a more financially and emotionally vulnerable environment for kids than is a two-parent home, and no amount of welfare money can change that. (Parents are not just cash machines.) A home with two unmarried natural parents is better than a single-parent home, but the evidence suggests that marriage is a more secure and durable arrangement than anything else. Cohabitation can certainly work, but if you are an embryo choosing your parents, and if all you know is that one couple is married and another is not, you'll go for the married couple every time. Marriage is the surest way to keep food on the table, to ensure against disasters and shocks, to weave your family into a supportive community, and to keep both parents involved in your upbringing. Senator Santorum was certainly right when he said that a healthy marriage is the best environment for childrearing.

Not only is marriage good for children; children are often good for marriage. Not always: research suggests that the arrival of children puts a heavy strain on many marriages. We have all heard stories about the couple with the difficult marriage who thought having a child would bring them closer together, only to end up divorced. But the divorce rate is slightly lower for couples with kids, possibly because children give even troubled couples a common project and a reason to put differences aside. If anything, marriage is more about children today than it ever was in the era when kids were viewed largely as farm hands or household labor, or as tokens of exchange in family deal making. In the educated classes, the child-centered marriage has reached the point where some couples do almost nothing that is not focused on rearing the perfect child. (In the old days, many children died, and so today's one-egg-in-one-basket strategy was impractical.) A lot of marriages nowadays are organized around the children, instead of the other way around.

Let no one say I deny that marriage is good for children and that children play a central role in marriage. If the harmony of sex, love, and marriage is a blessing, the harmony of sex, love, marriage, and children is, for most human beings, the greatest blessing of all.

To say that one is a blessing and the other a still greater blessing, however, is not to say that one is a blessing and the other a curse. Onward, then, to Proposition 2.

———

Without children, marriage isn't worth having. To put it another way, children are not just a blessing in marriage, and marriage is not just a blessing for children. Children are *essential* for marriage—not just one among many reasons but, as Santorum said, "*the* reason for marriage."

Obviously, in no way does this second proposition follow from the first. Shirts are uniquely good for covering arms, but it does not follow that armless people should not wear shirts. The fact that Proposition 2 in no way follows from Proposition 1 is reason enough to hold it in suspicion; to which may be added that it is preposterous. No one believes that childless marriages are illegitimate or bad for children or bad for matrimony: we honor and celebrate marriage whether children are in the picture or not. No law anywhere makes marriage contingent on the presence of minor children. One can hardly even imagine such a law. ("Dear Mr. and Mrs. Smith: This is to inform you that, because your children are now legal adults and you are past childbearing age, your marriage is officially dissolved.") According to the 2000 census, 54 percent of American married couples live in childless homes. Some homes are childless because the children are grown and gone, some because the couple never had children or married late in life (second marriages, for example). Does anybody, anywhere, think all those marriages should be forbidden?

Even if somebody did believe that childless marriages were worthless, the fact remains that many same-sex couples are not childless. If the presence of children is the qualification for the right to marry, then more than a quarter of same-sex couples qualify (according to the 2000 census). Those thousands of children in gay-couple households count, too. To cut them off from the benefits of marriage seems the height of capriciousness. I marvel, sometimes, at the ability of some same-sex-marriage opponents to extol marriage's benefits for children while managing never to see children in same-sex households. (And, no, wishing those children were in opposite-sex households is not an answer, it's a fantasy.)

No point dwelling here; or, really, on Proposition 3: *Without natural children, marriage isn't worth having.* Many children in gay households are adopted. Many are the natural children of one partner or the other, and join the couple through divorce or insemination or the other natural parent's death or whatever. None of them are the natural children of both parents, but I know of no one these days who thinks it is a good idea to regard adoptive children or their families as less in need of married parents. The arguments over gay adoption and custody are the subject for some other book. The point here is that you would be laughed out of town if you suggested that a heterosexual couple should be discouraged—to say nothing of banned—from getting married because their kids had other natural parents.

Instead of being laughed out of town, "married, without children" proponents make their stand on Proposition 4, which, I think, *should* be laughed out of town.

"It's about uniting together to be open to children," said Senator Santorum. Or, as I put what amounts to the same idea: *Without the possibility of natural children—the possibility of procreation—marriage isn't worth having.*

Here the thinking seems to be something like this: by their very nature, heterosexual relationships can and often do produce children. Put men and women together, and kids tend to come along. When kids come along, it's best for their parents to be married. Marriage is built on that biological truth. But homosexual relations are something different altogether. By their very nature, they cannot produce children. Natural children *never* come along. Extending marriage to people who cannot possibly have children together makes no sense. It makes a mockery of the core purpose of the institution. And society has no interest in it. In 1996, a commentator named Martin Mawyer made this point quite explicitly: "Government involves itself in the sacred union of marriage because of the *possibility* that marriage will produce children," he wrote (emphasis added). He continued:

> Between them, a same-sex couple is inherently incapable of creating offspring, and as such does not qualify for the benefits offered by the state to ease a family's burdens. Because of their inability to produce future generations, the community is under

no obligation and has no interest in placing homosexual relationships on the same pedestal as traditionally married couples. Simply put, the return on investment for the state is zero.

Considered glancingly, this view may make some intuitive sense. Plainly marriage and procreation and children have been linked since time immemorial, and plainly homosexual couples can't procreate. When you look more closely, however, the argument first collapses and then explodes, scorching the institution of marriage in the process. To be more specific: it is incoherent, incorrect, and antimarriage.

First, notice what the argument is not: a claim that the welfare of children is the basis of marriage. Santorum said, "It's about uniting together to be open to children," but same-sex unions are certainly "open to children." Kids come along in same-sex households all the time; they just are not conceived there. What Santorum really means, then, is that marriage must be open, not to children, but to procreation.

That, if you think about it, is not a child-centered view of marriage at all; it is a sex-centered view. It regards marriage's legitimacy as coming not from the presence or welfare of children but from the way the children got there.

Immediately, we hit a problem. What about heterosexual couples in which one or the other partner is sterile? There are millions of them, and they are no more capable of procreating than my partner, Michael, and I are. Some people are naturally infertile, some men and women have had themselves sterilized, some women have had hysterectomies, and of course women past menopause are infertile. Biologically speaking, a homosexual union is nothing but one variety of sterile union, and no different even in principle: a woman without a uterus is no more open to procreation than a man without a uterus.

It may sound like carping to stress the case of barren heterosexual marriage; the vast majority of first-time heterosexual newlyweds,

after all, can have children and probably will. But the point here
is fundamental. There are at least as many sterile heterosexual
couples in America as homosexual ones, and every one of them is
allowed to marry. If the possibility of procreation is what gives
meaning to marriage, then a postmenopausal woman who applies
for a marriage license should be turned away at the courthouse
door. What's more, she should be hooted at and condemned for
breaking the crucial link between marriage and procreation, for
stretching the meaning of marriage beyond all recognition, and
for reducing the institution to frivolity. The Family Research
Council, Focus on the Family, and Concerned Women for America should point at her and say, "If she can marry, why not
polygamy? Why not marriage to pets?"

Curiously, they do not say that. Their real position is that the
possibility of procreation defines marriage when homosexuals are
involved, but not when heterosexuals are involved. To put the
point more starkly, sterility disqualifies *all* homosexuals from
marriage, but it disqualifies *no* heterosexuals. So the distinction
is not pro-procreation (much less pro-children) at all. It is merely
antihomosexual.

That is why the "possibility of natural children" argument is
incoherent, to say nothing of unfair (and not just to same-sex
couples but also to their kids). But it is also incorrect. When an
aging widow takes a second husband, people don't say, "Well,
that's too bad, because it loosens the bond between marriage and
procreation, but I guess we've got to let her do it." They say,
"Good for her! Congratulations! Hallelujah!" Not only is the
notion that the community and the state have no stake in this
woman's marriage incorrect; everyone who has ever celebrated
the wedding of a postmenopausal woman knows it is incorrect.

The reason, of course, is that marriage is about children but not
only about children. It is also about happiness, security, safety,
prosperity, good health, sound mind, altruism, personal growth, sex
(the elderly have it, too), and—did I almost forget to mention?—

love. A state which takes no interest in helping citizens and communities secure those benefits is a very shortsighted state indeed—which may be why no such state exists. I have never heard of any jurisdiction anywhere which either conditions marriage on fertility or imagines that doing so would be a sane public policy. (Write me if I'm wrong.)

To exclude homosexuals, people who hold to the possibility-of-procreation line cannot just say that procreation is one of a number of justifications for marriage. They have to say it is the *only* justification, or at least the only one worth bothering with, because all the rest—providing caregivers, domesticating young adults, bolstering economic security, looking after children—can apply to homosexuals. But then, having said that the possibility of procreation is the only rationale for marriage, they immediately sabotage even that rationale by refusing to apply it to sterile heterosexuals. Here is where the possibility-of-procreation argument turns destructive: in its fixation on excluding homosexuals, it leaves no consistent rationale for the privileged status of heterosexual marriage. Its advocates tear away any coherent foundation which secular marriage might have—precisely the opposite of what they claim they want to do. If they have to undercut marriage to save it from the homosexuals, so be it!

The resulting message is not just peculiar, it is antimarriage. If you say that marriage without the possibility of procreation isn't worth having, you also say, "We don't care if people who can't conceive kids shack up instead of marrying. Their marriages are worthless anyway. We don't care if they divorce, either. Their commitment is meaningless from society's point of view." I can't think of a worse message for marriage. Or a sillier one.

Mercifully, the possibility-of-procreation crowd is only kidding. In my years of discussing same-sex marriage, I have encountered only two people who seriously suggested that, in an ideal world, sterility should be a bar to marriage. One was a young editor on the staff of a conservative magazine, who got himself cornered in a talk-radio debate. The other is the aforementioned Martin Mawyer, who wrote in his 1996 article that sterile heterosexuals should be allowed to marry only because administering fertility tests would be intrusive. Everyone else either squirms or changes the subject.

In the squirming category are people who say, as I suspect Senator Santorum might, something like: "Look here, I'm not unreasonable. I'm saying that there is something unique and special about a procreative marriage, not that nonprocreative marriages have nothing to offer. My heart goes out to people in infertile marriages. It isn't their fault that they can't have kids, and it doesn't make their marriage worthless. But, let's face it, a procreative marriage is the ideal. It is what the institution was designed for and it is what we aim for."

All well and good—but no help at all, because one can, and I think should, make precisely the same point about same-sex unions. Even if you believe nonprocreative marriage cannot be as good as procreative marriage, that is no reason to ban it, much less to ban it inconsistently (only for homosexuals). Softening the argument, in that sense, only sharpens the blow, because it heightens the contrast between the sympathetic and supportive treatment that barren heterosexual marriages receive and the flat legal prohibition of homosexual marriages. When I see a heterosexual couple who have made a successful marriage despite being unable to have children, I see their devotion as, if anything, all the more admirable. Anyway, the last thing I would think to do is disparage their marriage as frivolous or unworthy, and I can't imagine regarding it with hostility. Why treat homosexual unions with any less compassion?

Another squirm: "But all homosexual unions are sterile. Only some heterosexual ones are. For heterosexuals, barrenness is the exception. For homosexuals, it is the rule." Again, no help, unless you think homosexual individuals don't matter as much as infertile heterosexual individuals do. After all, postmenopausal women are also a barren class—and a large one. No one lumps them together and says, "None of them can procreate. We have to shut them out to defend the link between marriage and procreation." Imagine if infertile heterosexuals all developed a birthmark on their forehead, making them easily identifiable as a class. Would anybody favor barring them from marriage? Would anyone even think of it?

At this point, some people just throw up their hands. Thus William Bennett, in *The Broken Hearth:*

> Well, rejoin homosexual rights activists, if procreation is central to marriage, then for the sake of consistency we should not allow sterile or older couples to marry, either. As debater's points go, this is exceptionally weak. *One can believe that procreation is a primary purpose of marriage without insisting that only people who can and will have children be allowed to marry.* Aristotle defined nature as "that which is, always or for the most part." A person may be born without a hand, but it remains natural that humans have two hands; a dog with three legs is still a member of the natural category of four-legged creatures. Just so, heterosexual couples who remain childless do not violate the norm, or change the essence, of marriage. Two men who marry do. [Italics added.]

Right you are, Mr. Bennett. Just because procreation is a purpose of marriage doesn't mean that only fertile couples should be allowed to marry. Infertile couples, including gay couples, should be allowed to marry, too. But it appears that, with all this talk of procreation and marriage, we were just wasting our time. The real reason homosexual couples can't marry is that their marrying would violate the very definition ("essence") of marriage, which is that . . . only heterosexual couples can marry! At long last, who knows how many words later, we are back where we started: at "because I said so" or "because God or nature said so" or, really, "because you just can't."

———

In fairness, Bennett and others who fall back on appeals to nature are not without a reasoned argument. Marriage, they say, is about the natural complementarity of the sexes, as evinced by the fact that only a male-female couple can have children. But this is, in fact, the most peculiar and strained argument of all. We come, then, to Proposition 5: *Without sex of the* type *which produces children, marriage isn't worth having.*

It is true, runs the argument, that many heterosexuals can't procreate. But they can have penile-vaginal intercourse; and although procreation will not result, penile-vaginal intercourse is the one *type* of union which produces children; therefore it is the only basis for a proper marriage; therefore civil marriage between people who cannot have penile-vaginal intercourse should be against the law.

As Anna Russell, the British comedienne, used to say of the plots of Wagner's operas: I am not making this up. When I state the case as bluntly as I just did, most people would not give it the time of day. Usually, however, it is dressed up in fancy verbiage, with phrases like "one-flesh communion," "natural teleology of the body," "biological complementarity," "single reproductive principle," "procreative significance," "two-in-one-flesh common good," and so forth.

Notice, here, how far we have come from regarding marriage as being about children. Now it is not about children per se, nor about how the children got there, nor even about biology (penises and vaginas do not unite biologically; sperm and egg do). It is about heterosexuality, pure and simple. In effect, it is about having the equipment for penile-vaginal intercourse. To be sure, the proponents of this argument do not frame it quite that way. They speak, as Bennett did in a 2003 *Los Angeles Times* article, of "the inescapable fact of nature that we are created male and female," and of "a natural sexual order," and of spouses being "complementary on the basis of nature." But nowadays marriages are founded primarily on the complementarity of individuals, not sexes; and, as we know from the high divorce rate, many male-female couples turn out not to be very complementary at all. Moreover, homosexuals exist. Clearly a gay man and a lesbian would not be sexually complementary in any sense that mattered. On analysis, then, "complementary" turns out to mean nothing more than that the pair is capable of heterosexual intercourse.

Bennett accuses what he calls "the homosexual vanguard" (thanks, I guess) of wanting to "replace sexual identity . . . with sexual behavior as a fundamental organizing principle of society." This is an odd accusation, because defining marriage strictly in terms of sexual capacity—specifically, the capacity for penile-vaginal intercourse—is precisely what *he* is doing. Most Americans, the homosexual vanguard included, see marriage as being more about commitment and self-restraint and family and love than about what kind of sexual equipment you have. Why, one wonders, would marriage's self-styled defenders be reducing marriage, in its very essence, to—forgive my bluntness—man-boinks-woman? Well, here is a guess: by locating the essence of marriage in the one type of sex which homosexuals cannot have, they finally manage to draw a line which includes all straight unions in the proper domain of matrimony, while excluding all gay ones. If they have to trivialize marriage in order to save it from the homosexuals—so be it!

The reason the "procreative-type sex" view gets any hearing at all today is historical. As E. J. Graff explains in *What Is Marriage For?*, Christianity, when it came along, was unusual in its sexual asceticism. Judaism, for example, regards pleasure-seeking sex as a good thing, even an obligation which a man owes to a woman, provided that the sex takes place only in marriage and that it supplements but does not supplant procreative sex. (The early rabbis may have figured that pleasure-seeking spouses would have more babies. No dummies, those rabbis.) Early Christians, however, believed the end of the world would soon come, and so procreating was not a priority. Christianity saw celibacy, the giving of oneself over to God,

as the noblest life, and sexual relations as a compromise necessary for the making of more human beings. Nonprocreative sex
was an abuse of the instruments God made for procreation. If sex
did not happen to produce a pregnancy, that was one thing; but if
you were deliberately avoiding a pregnancy, that was wicked. And
this was true whether you were married or not. For a married couple
to have contracepted sex was to turn the bridal chamber into a
brothel. In that respect, homosexual sex, masturbation, and contraception were all sodomitic, or "vices against nature." By contrast, sex in a sterile marriage was fine (without contraception, of
course), because you never know: a baby just might happen. Still,
Graff notes, "For many centuries the Church refused to bless
remarrying widows and widowers, especially if the woman was too
old to bear children."

For somebody raised Jewish, as I was, this whole sex-must-be-
procreative rigmarole seems nothing more than a sectarian curios-
ity: something which Catholics have every right to believe but
which need not detain anybody else, and which today even most
American Catholics probably do not accept. It embodies nothing
more than the theology of one religion, and it depends for its
coherence on a belief in miracles (but if God could miraculously
bring forth a baby from a sterile heterosexual couple, why not from
a homosexual one?—oh, never mind). It has no business determining what secular law should be. We are talking, after all, about
whether same-sex marriage should be legal, not about what type
of sex is best in God's eyes. To a surprising extent, advocates of the
procreative-type-sex view forget altogether about the distinction,
or else they deliberately elide it. I'll leave you to decide which of
those is going on here (from an article by William E. May, published in 2003 in the *Washington Times*):

Genital coition is the only bodily act intrinsically capable of
generating new human life. Kissing, holding hands, fondling,
and anal-oral sex cannot generate children. . . . The marital

union of a man and a woman who have given themselves unre-
servedly in marriage and who can consummate their union in a
beautiful bodily act of conjugal intercourse is the best place to
serve as a "home" for new human life. . . . A marriage of this
kind contributes uniquely to the common good. *It merits legal
protection*; same-sex unions are not the same, and, sadly,
merely mimic the real thing. [Italics added.]

Notice how casually the author has skipped from saying that
"genital coition" is morally special all the way to saying that marriages without the possibility of genital coition should be illegal.

Most Americans today are reluctant to smuggle a sectarian theology into law; and, of course, where heterosexuals are concerned,
they long ago relinquished any idea that nonprocreative sex is
wicked. They decided instead that "kissing, holding hands,
fondling, and anal-oral sex" can bring not only pleasure but heightened intimacy, and they partook vigorously. They stopped crusad-
ing against contraception as a threat to marriage (if they ever had)
and began seeing it as virtually a marital necessity; and then, in
the 1960s, they recognized a constitutional right to use it. The
few people who take the view that marriage is worth having only
if it has the possibility of procreative-type sex, and not otherwise,
are in effect saying that homosexuals are to be the unwilling last
subjects of canon law. Thanks, but no thanks.

———

The remaining avenue open to people in the marriage-is-for-
procreation camp is simply to acknowledge that they are setting up
a double standard. In effect, they are demanding (not asking) of
gays a special sacrifice. Call it the one-last-horse argument. For
example, in an editorial published in 2003, *National Review* said:
"Traditionally, marriage has been understood to be ordered to
procreation." Fair enough. "It was understood that the ideal setting for the rearing of children was the marriage of their parents."

Again, fair enough. The editorialist goes on to note, quite rightly, that the ideal could not always be achieved and then was directly challenged, for instance by "the widespread practice of divorce and remarriage," and also by "such seemingly marginal developments as the rise of sperm banks." All of those things, of course, are already legal. But "gay marriage would cut the last cord which ties marriage to the well-being of children. It is a step we should not take."

Set aside the obvious rejoinder that if "the well-being of children" is the issue, then marriage should be encouraged rather than banned for same-sex couples with kids. Assume that *National Review*'s editorialist was actually talking about the tying of marriage to procreation and not to the well-being of children. The larger argument here is that heterosexuals have done all kinds of things to weaken the ties between fertility (or children) and marriage, but at least, by stopping same-sex marriage, we can avoid letting this one last horse out of the barn.

I would take the one-last-horse argument more seriously if its advocates showed more concern for the welfare of the horse. I might even settle for any concern at all. It would be one thing if they went to gay America on bended knee and said, "We know that all heterosexuals can be legally married, no questions asked, whether or not they do or will or even can have children. We know that, in straight America, marriage and procreation were legally and morally detached years ago. But we have a bad situation in this country. Too many people have forgotten about the link between marriage and kids. And no way will the heterosexual majority ever give up easy divorce or legal contraception or anything else. So here's the deal. Having really messed things up, we heterosexuals are hoping you gay folks will help us out. We're asking you to give up any hope of marriage. We're asking the kids in your homes to do without married parents. That's a hardship, for sure, but in exchange we will present every gay American with a medal, designate a national Gay Patriots Day, and—oh, right—let gay couples share health insurance and frequent-flier miles."

Dream on. Instead, we get that lazy Long Dark Age assumption that the welfare of gay families (and of the children in them) is a commodity to be spent by heterosexuals. If I sound bitter, I don't mean to. I don't think the one-last-horsers are being deliberately callous. I think they simply are not in the habit of thinking of homosexuals as their equals.

In fairness, same-sex marriage is a reform, a big reform, and to most people it is a radical change. In a country with more than its share of divorce and illegitimacy and deadbeat dads, I cannot and do not expect gay marriage as a matter of right. So it behooves me to point out that the one-last-horse argument is weak even on its own terms. The conservative commentator Maggie Gallagher observes, "I am sure unisex marriage will dramatically affect the cultural norms and values of the next generation in ways which will encourage divorce and disconnect marriage further from childrearing." The idea here seems to be that fertile straight couples are more likely to get or stayed married for their children's sake if they know that childless homosexual couples cannot get married at all. This seems peculiar, to say the least. One might as well say that the way to encourage people who own guns to take firearms-safety classes is by forbidding people who don't own guns to take firearms-safety classes. Another way to see the logical problem with the notion that fertile people will be more likely to marry if infertile people cannot is to ask: If, starting tomorrow, we banned infertile heterosexuals from marrying and told them they all had to shack up instead, would that reduce the divorce rate? The illegitimacy rate? Would it make young couples less likely to cohabit? Would it be good for children? For marriage? Actually, the main result would be to ensure that a lot of adopted children would grow up with unmarried parents—precisely what is happening in gay households right now.

At bottom, the problem with the one-last-horse argument is that the other horses were never in the barn to begin with, and keeping that one queer horse locked up in there won't help corral them. Straight marriage has never been conditioned on procreation or children, and therefore saying that only gays can't marry sends a message not that marriage and kids go together but that marriage and gays don't go together—even when gays have kids! Perhaps that is the real agenda. I leave you to decide.

————

Until now, a great many people have taken for granted that to be antigay is the same thing as to be promarriage (or profamily). Until recently, after all, homosexuals were presumed not to exist, so homosexuality was presumed to be a grotesque substitute for heterosexual family life. "It's common sense that a marriage is between a man and a woman," Senator Santorum said. "I mean, every civilization in the history of man has recognized a unique bond."

Marriage is indeed a unique bond, but in what does its uniqueness consist? Marriage now can be unique because it is the gold standard for commitment, or it can be unique because it is the only kind of bond which excludes homosexuals. It can be society's way of saying to a newlywed couple, "Thank goodness you've formed a family," or it can be society's way of saying, "Thank goodness you're not gay," but it can no longer be both. Memo to friends of marriage and family: the river of history has turned. This choice is important. Get it right.

7

Anything Goes

If marriage is redefined to include two men in love," wrote the conservative columnist Charles Krauthammer in July 1996, "on what possible grounds can it be denied to three men in love?" Marriage, he declared in a *Time* magazine article, is two-sex for the same reasons—tradition, religion, utility, morality—that it is two-person. "Not good enough reasons, say the gay activists. No? Then show me yours for opposing polygamy and incest."

With that counterchallenge of his own, he met the challenge which Barney Frank had put to his colleagues on the House floor only a few days before. Frank had wanted to know: Why does the health of marriage depend on the exclusion of a small number of homosexuals? Instead of focusing, as people who link marriage to procreation do, on the "homosexual" part of Frank's question, Krauthammer and others who raised what I call the anything-goes argument focused on the "exclusion" part. If, they argued, homosexual couples could not be excluded, then it would prove impossible to exclude anyone who wanted to marry any number of any sort of people—or even (a few grumbled) any sort of nonpeople, such as pets. Once the door was opened to male-male and female-female couples, polygamy, incest, even bestiality would be next.

In this chapter, I will leave aside the bestiality claim, because I don't know of any serious thinker who makes it and because the arguments I will make against the polygamy and incest claims are more than strong enough to deal with bestiality. The Krauthammer challenge, however, must not be set aside. It rivals the "it's about procreation" argument in prevalence and is much more cogent. One hears it again and again. "If gay marriage, what's next? Pretty soon, anything goes."

Is same-sex marriage a Pandora's box, releasing a swarm of progressively more radical redefinitions of marriage? Or is it, by contrast, more like a lock on the box, a change which is logically and politically unlike any of those others, one whose approval would, if anything, help draw a line against them?

The anything-goes argument really breaks down into two interwoven but different kinds of claims. Most people do not bother to distinguish them, because they make the two claims as a package, but it is important to sort them out. The first is the claim that same-sex marriage and other potential changes in marriage's boundaries—to include polygamy or incest—are logically related. That is, if you accept the premises of one, you have no principled grounds upon which to oppose the others. The second is the claim that same-sex marriage and the others are politically or psychologically related. That is, as a practical matter, once you have launched one reform, you will soften the public's political and mental resistance to all the others.

Is either claim right? Are both?

———

In 2003, Senator Rick Santorum made the case for a logical connection between same-sex marriage and polygamy as succinctly as anyone has. "It's not to affirm the love of two people," he said. "I mean, that's not what marriage is about. I mean, if that were the case, then lots of different people and lots of different combinations could be, quote, 'married.'"

Santorum seems to be analyzing the situation as follows: all Americans today enjoy the right to marry someone of the opposite sex. The law treats everyone alike, in that respect, and so rests in equilibrium. Homosexuals have come along with an assertion which would upset the equilibrium. They say marriage is about affirming one's love, whatever that happens to be. Well, some people fall in love with more than one person. Some people fall in love with their close kin. Some people might even claim to fall in love with their pets, and who could disprove such a claim? Once we establish the principle that two men can marry just because they love each other, we have affirmed the principle that you can marry anyone you love. Then, on the liberal principle of equal treatment, polygamists will say, "What about us? Affirm our love, too." And, having yielded the basic principle (marry whomever you love), we'll have no grounds to refuse.

Note, here, that the argument rests on two premises, not just one. The first is that homosexuals and polygamists or incestuists (as I'll call them) are comparably situated. Admit one group, and you logically need to admit the other. The second is that there are no separate reasons, unrelated to same-sex marriage, to oppose polygamy or incest. *Both* premises need to stand if "anything goes" is to stand. One domino cannot tip another, after all, if the two are a mile apart or if the second one is propped up independently. As it happens, both premises are wrong.

Santorum and the others have misanalyzed the situation. Gay people are not asking for the legal right to marry anybody they love or everybody they love. That would indeed be a radical transformation of the boundary of marriage, or really an erasure of the boundary altogether. Instead, homosexuals are asking for what all heterosexuals possess already: the legal right to marry *somebody* they love.

Heterosexuals, of course, cannot marry anyone or everyone they love. They cannot marry their sister or a group of two or three people. But they can all marry one person they love, and the pool of potential mates is very large: half the world's population minus one's own immediate family. One person, one partner—that is not quite anybody, but it is plenty of choice, enough so that most people have good odds of marrying.

I suppose some polygamists might claim they are not comparably treated, but the claim is very hard to maintain with a straight face. Any man who can fall in love with two women can fall in love with each of them, and in fact has already done so. And this happens all the time. About a quarter of the world's romantic novels and songs would disappear if their writers had to get by without romantic triangles—men and women torn between two lovers. Moreover, the law has no beef with people loving, and having sex with, more than one person at a time. Splitting one's affections may be foolish or hurtful, but it is common and legal. All the law says is that you can *marry* only one of the people you love. So polygamists have plenty of people they can marry. In a sense, their problem is that they have too many marriage candidates, and they would prefer not to narrow the field down to one.

I do not actually know of any advocates of incestuous marriage, but if there were any, they might try to claim that they, too, are cut off from marital fulfillment, but again their claim is hard to take seriously. I have never heard anyone claim that there is a group of human beings so constituted as to be able to love and bond erotically and romantically only with a parent or a sibling. To my knowledge, no such specimen has ever made itself known to science. It may occur, as a matter of happenstance, that once in a great while someone falls in love romantically with a sibling or a parent, but that only means those people have made the one selection in a billion which the law does not accommodate. Many of us happen to fall in love with people whom, for whatever reason, we can't marry: people who are already married, for example, or people who do not reciprocate our love, or people who live in a Tibetan monastery. The law's interest is only in making sure that, in a world full of romantic disappointment, we can all find plenty of other candidates if our first choice falls through.

If, therefore, the rule is that the law should give everyone a realistic hope of marrying *somebody* he loves—not zero people, not two people, not three people, but one person—there is no other group in the country whose situation is comparable to homosexuals', because only homosexuals are barred, by law, from marrying *anyone* they love. The gay situation is unique. It is not that gays have to settle for their second or third choice. It is that gay people's set of choices is the null set. Zero. For the typical human being, who needs companionship and love and someone to come home to, zero is too few by a factor of infinity.

And so a homosexual woman who wants to marry one unrelated woman is not logically equivalent to a heterosexual woman who wants to marry her two neighbors or her brother or her dog or her Volkswagen. She is like a heterosexual woman who wants to marry one unrelated man. Whereas the law allows the heterosexual woman to marry somebody she loves, it forbids the homosexual woman to do precisely the same thing.

Will allowing everyone to marry somebody leave us without a principled reply to someone who wants to marry anyone or everyone? No: no more than giving every woman one vote left no principled answer to men who might then have demanded two votes. The easiest reply to "anything goes," then, is that I need not reply at all, except to say: when heterosexuals get the right to marry two other people or a sibling or a dog or a Volkswagen, homosexuals should get that right also. Until then, there is no reason to discuss it.

————

The easy reply, though, seems a bit of a dodge, especially if polygamists or incestuists press their case. They might say, "Sure, our situation is not strictly comparable to gays', but you stretched to accommodate them, and for us a plural marriage or an incestuous marriage is a better, happier way of life. So why don't you stretch to accommodate us as well? It may not be logically required, but it is the compassionate thing to do."

One of the most curious aspects of the anything-goes argument is that it implicitly gives away the store, particularly to the polygamists. It says not just that same-sex marriage leads logically to plural marriage, but that there are no good reasons other than blind adherence to tradition to oppose plural marriage. Consider, for example, this quotation from an article by Hadley Arkes, a scholar who opposes same-sex marriage:

> The traditional understanding of marriage is grounded in the "natural teleology of the body"—in the inescapable fact that only a man and a woman, and only two people, not three, can generate a child. Once marriage is detached from that natural teleology of the body, what ground of principle would thereafter confine marriage to two people rather than some larger grouping?

Actually, the fact that only a man and a woman can create a child has never been the slightest impediment to polygamy; hundreds of human cultures, after all, have been polygamous, but none have had legal same-sex marriage. Men have been perfectly happy to marry as many women as they can have children with. That's a quibble, though. More important is to see that Arkes's statement is a good example of some conservatives' tendency to throw away some of the strongest rationales for marriage's special prestige in order to keep homosexuals out. In fact, society and the state have strong reasons to frown upon and, yes, forbid polygamous and incestuous marriage, and those reasons are just as strong in a world with same-sex marriage as in a world without it.

I mentioned in chapter 1 that the large majority of known human cultures have been polygamous—meaning, strictly speaking, polygynous (one man, several wives), because polyandry (one woman, several husbands) is vanishingly rare. Yet as far as I can tell not a single one of those polygamous societies has ever been a liberal democracy. (Let me know if I missed one somewhere.) To the contrary, they tend to be authoritarian rather than liberal, hierarchical and male-supremacist rather than egalitarian, and closed rather than open. Examples begin with the biblical patriarchs and extend through Brigham Young's Mormons down to Saudi Arabia today. Why?

As a mathematical necessity (given that polyandry is extremely rare), for one man to have two wives means that some other man will have none. Moreover, the higher a man's status, the more wives he gets. As a status symbol, a yacht or a Lamborghini can't hold a candle to a harem. With elite men taking more than their share, low-status men have trouble finding mates, and some can't marry at all. This problem is not just theoretical. In developing countries where girls are disproportionately aborted, shortages of brides for young men lead to an array of intractable social problems. By taking more women than men off the marriage market, polygamy has much the same result.

Whether in the Third World or in inner-city America, a good way to create an angry and restless underclass is to create a population of unmarriageable, low-status men. In chapter 1, I cited evidence that young, unmarried men are three times more likely than are comparable married men to commit murder, and they are also more likely to rob and rape. To worsen the problem by an order of magnitude, make these young men not only unmarried but unmarriageable. Force them to go through life unmarried, at the bottom of a status hierarchy, peering up resentfully at elite men with one or more wives on each arm. The practical fact, I suspect, is that such a society can keep a lid on its marriageless underclass only by repressing it. Every man needs to know his place and be kept in it, by convention if possible, by force if necessary.

I can't prove it, but I think the one-person-one-spouse rule is an essential step on the path to liberal democracy, because it is the only rule which opens marriage to everybody. Without equal-opportunity marriage, anything like today's social mobility and political equality would be unthinkable. Women, especially, would be the losers, because in polygamous marriages they often become more like their husband's rival concubines than his full equals.

It's tempting to retort, "All of that might be true in a society where polygamy was widely practiced. But in modern America, what harm does it do if a few people here and there take multiple spouses?" The answer goes back to Immanuel Kant, one of the touchstone theorists of modern liberalism. A liberal society, he said, needs to insist on rules that work at least as well when applied to everybody as when applied to only a few. Otherwise the government ends up picking and choosing favored citizens. When a first-grade teacher says, "The reason you can't take two jars of paint, Tommy, is that if everyone took two jars we wouldn't have enough to go around," she is inculcating the basic Kantian principle of legislating for equality.

We can't assume that polygamy would remain rare if it were legalized; but we also could not very well say, "The first 1 percent of the population who want polygamous marriages can have them, but after that, the door is shut." Creating a form of marriage in the hope that hardly anyone would use it seems unwise, to put it mildly. And note that even small numbers of polygamous marriages would not necessarily be harmless. Unless every polygamous marriage were balanced by a polyandrous one—which is culturally unprecedented, and which no law could control—for each additional woman in a polygamous marriage there would be one man, probably at the bottom of the totem pole, who would have to do without marriage. If you think this is no cause for concern, ask yourself how many more poor or disadvantaged young men should come of age in a world where finding marriage is hard but finding sex is easy.

For real sticklers, one question remains. "Couldn't at least *gay* people form plural marriages without doing society any harm?

After all, they aren't limited to an equal number of opposite-sex partners." I could say all kinds of things by way of reply, but the best reply may be: don't be ridiculous. Gay people want equal rights, not special rights; straight people want to give gay people equal rights, not special rights; creating an entirely new form of marriage just for homosexuals would serve no social purpose except to erode the norm of monogamy and bolster the stereotype of homosexual freakishness; and, last but not least, America will legalize gays-only polygamy at about the same time as monkeys fly out of my ear.

Before we leave planet Earth altogether, a reality check. From society's point of view, the main purpose of marriage is not, and never has been, to affirm love, as Rick Santorum so aptly said. If the social point of marriage were to let everybody seek his ultimate amorous fulfillment, then adultery would be a standard part of the marital package. But neither is marriage's purpose to exclude homosexuals; nor is its *only* purpose to create a healthy environment for childrearing. Another essential social purpose of secular marriage, rather, is to bond as many people as possible into committed, stable relationships. Such societies-within-society—we call them families—are not only good for children (including children in gay-couple households); they are vitally important for adults. A sensible society seeks to stabilize and nurture as many people as possible. A liberal society seeks to make the good life available to as many people as possible. Same-sex marriage accords with both of those aspirations. Polygamy wrecks them.

———

And now, a few words about incestuous marriage. Just a few, because I know of no demand for it.

Incest, of course, may produce impaired children: birth defects, retardation, genetic diseases. That is obviously a concern, but it applies to incestuous sex rather than incestuous marriage as such. Incestuous marriage is a dreadful idea for a different reason, one which holds even for sterile and homosexual couples. Imagine a society where parents and children viewed each other as potential mates. Just for a start, many children would grow up wondering whether their parents had sexual designs on them, or were grooming them as a potential spouse. Holding open the prospect of incestuous marriage would devastate family life by legitimizing sexual predation within it.

Note that this is true even though incestuous marriage would be limited to adults. Imagine being a fourteen-year-old girl and suspecting that your sixteen-year-old brother or thirty-four-year-old father had ideas about courting you in a few years. Imagine being the sixteen-year-old boy and developing what you think is a crush on your younger sister and being able to fantasize and talk about marrying her someday. Imagine being the parent and telling your son he can marry his sister someday, but right now he needs to keep his hands off her. My guess is that a conscientious parent would feel obliged to separate the siblings, and that if the parent didn't separate them, quite a few would run away. Truly, though, I cannot fathom all the effects which the prospect of child-parent or sibling-sibling marriage might have on the dynamics of family life, but I can't imagine that the effects would be good, and I can't imagine why anyone would want to try the experiment and see.

Needless to say, same-sex marriage, raises no such concerns. Also needless to say, homosexual incestuous marriage would be just as bad as heterosexual incestuous marriage and should be just as illegal. Also needless to say, it is an option no one needs and no one even seems to want. Needless to say, enough said.

––––––

"No one ever went broke underestimating the intelligence of the American people." So goes the old adage, and so a number of critics of same-sex marriage seem to believe. Well, old adages stay in circulation for a reason, and sensible policy makers try to plan for mistakes and political cave-ins. So the political, practical argument which links gay marriage to a stream of other, less desirable (or, if you prefer, *even* less desirable) changes deserves a hearing.

Granted (goes the argument), from a logical point of view, gay marriage and polygamous marriage or incestuous marriage are more like opposites than equivalents. But the American public cannot be counted on to follow intricate logical arguments, especially since people will be prevailed upon by opportunistic sloganeering with words like "love" and "compassion" and "equality." Politically speaking, traditional marriage is a boulder perched on an outcropping. Push it, and you can't be sure which way it might roll. Part of what keeps polygamy off the political radar—part of the reason there is hardly any noticeable constituency for it—is the perceived difficulty in making any fundamental change in the definition of marriage. If same-sex marriage were legalized, the boulder would start to roll. Polygamists (or polyamorists, as proponents of plural marriage often call themselves) would see a chance to blur the line between marriage and a group arrangement, and, with gays having won a momentous reform, no one would be in a position to tell them to take a hike.

In *The Weekly Standard* in 2003, Stanley Kurtz, a prominent and thoughtful opponent of gay marriage, quoted a law professor named David Chambers as having written (hopefully), "By ceasing to conceive of marriage as a partnership composed of one person of each sex, the state may become more receptive to units of three or more." Kurtz commented: "Gradual transition from gay marriage to state-sanctioned polyamory, and the eventual abolition of marriage itself as a legal category, is now the most influential paradigm within academic family law." Other observers say the radicals are a fringe group, even in the academic world. However, assume for argument's sake that the radicals are out there and that they see gay marriage as the thin edge of the wedge and that they will have at least some influence. Then the question is: If legalizing polygamy is a bad idea, what is the best way to stop it from happening? The conservative answer seems to be: stop *any-thing* from happening, beginning with gay marriage. Do not open the front door even a crack. Throw your body and all the furniture in front of it.

What such conservatives forget is the back door. A brief recap of the points I made in chapter 5 may be useful here. History's river has rounded a bend and homosexuals are here for good, both in the sense that they are not going to return to hiding and in the sense that their sexuality is broadly recognized as an unchosen and fundamental part of their makeup. Moreover, society's interest in stabilizing gay people's lives is powerful, and Americans are compassionate, and over time gay couples will establish themselves as fixtures of American life. If society does not make a place for gay couples inside marriage, gay couples will make a place for themselves in society outside marriage, by means of public civil-union programs, private domestic-partner benefits, and socially blessed cohabitation—all of which will be tempting and increasingly common alternatives for heterosexuals. The choice is not gay marriage or nothing. It is gay marriage or a bunch of nonmarital alternatives.

So the wise policy maker, looking ahead, asks the next question. Which social institution will be more resistant to the pryings and pleadings of polygamists: marriage or something else? Marriage is an ancient institution of great cultural and legal and religious importance, which is exactly why the gay-marriage debate touches such deep chords. Almost by definition, any major change to marriage will create a stir, with lots of attention and public debate. It is true that legalization of same-sex marriage might lessen resistance to other forms of change. Consider, however, the alternative. Civil unions and domestic-partner programs are newfangled designations which governments and corporate human-resources departments just made up. That's the whole point: these new arrangements aren't encumbered with a lot of cultural baggage. When polyamorists come and ask for three-way

health benefits, the human resources department or city government might say, "That's too expensive," but they won't be able to
say, "It has never been done before and now isn't the time to
start," because the domestic-partner program was just invented
the day before yesterday. The polygamist would say, "Look, this
program isn't marriage anyway—that's why it exists. I have two
equally important women in my life, and we all share a home and
depend on one another, and hardly anyone else is in this position.
So have a heart and sign up both of my girlfriends for domestic-
partner benefits."

It all might stop there. Or it might not. To whatever extent
society bestows recognition and legitimacy and prerogatives on
group arrangements, the path would be eased for the law to follow suit. Group marriage might come to seem a less shocking
arrangement. A generation on, adjusting legal marriage to allow
groups might seem a natural thing to do. Of course, opponents
would point out the dangers. I certainly plan to. But the psycho-
logical argument cuts both ways. If the problem is that, once
people get used to reforming marriage, any reform could lead to
every reform, then surely the social sanction of polygamous pseudomarriage is at least as likely to lead toward polygamy as is the legal
sanction of monogamous gay marriage. To whatever extent gay
marriage gives polygamists a foot in the front door, the alternatives to gay marriage give them a whole leg in the back door.

I am not predicting any of this. I doubt that the radicals will get
very far in any event, because Americans are a basically sensible
people. One point, however, is clear. Nonmarriage and pseudomarriage are much easier targets for polygamists and other radicals than marriage is. Polyamory advocates may be out there, but it
is an illusion to think that the ban on same-sex marriage will slow
them down.

I can see the rejoinder forming on your lips. "Aha! Rauch has
just inadvertently explained why it is so important to leave the
definition of marriage alone. Marriage is hard to change, as he

concedes—as, in fact, he trumpets. The thing to do is leave it
that way. If family radicals want to set up three-way marriage-lite,
we'll just have to fight that fight when the time comes. The critical thing is to make sure that whatever they fiddle with is not
marriage." So we're back to ABM: whatever else you do, don't
mess with marriage. Fight the polygamists on other turf.

This ABMer could go a twist further and really nail me. "In
fact," he could say, "Rauch's argument is self-defeating. He
depends on marriage's tamper resistance to stop polygamy, even as
he calls for just the sort of radical redefinition which would make
marriage less tamper resistant. He's really saying: 'One unprecedented, dramatic change—then no more.' But that's not how
things work. In the real world, break one taboo, and others follow."

Well, that seems a strong point. I can't count on marriage to ward
off future reformers while I'm busy reforming it myself. Can I?

———

Yes, I can. For this reason: not all reforms are alike. In this case,
they could hardly be more different.

What we are really disputing here is where marriage should
make its stand. I mean its political stand, but I also mean the
principle it seeks to defend. If you want to resist polygamists who
might be out there—and who presumably will be out there
whether or not you allow same-sex marriage—what is the high-
est, driest, firmest ground for marriage to be on? The ABMer says
the principle marriage defends should be: "Don't change marriage." I say the principle should be: "One person, one spouse."

And that, of course, is precisely the principle of same-sex marriage: everyone should have a reasonable chance of marrying
somebody, as opposed to nobody or everybody or anybody. Why,
conservatives might ask themselves, is America debating gay marriage seriously in the first place? Why does the idea have any traction at all? The answer is that, in a liberal society which recognizes
that homosexuals exist, many people feel instinctively that "zero"

is the wrong answer to the question "How many people should a homosexual be able to marry?" Gay marriage is on the agenda precisely because it aligns with the one-person-one-partner rule. It extends and universalizes the existing principle. It thus allows advocates of the one-person-one-partner rule to defend monogamous marriage without hypocrisy or inconsistency. It clarifies rather than smudges marriage's boundaries by confirming marriage as *the* one-to-one lifelong commitment of choice.

My contention is that polyamorists and other reformers who want to define any group or union as a marriage, to the extent they look scary at all, look scary because marriage today is on illiberal and thus unstable ground. If polyamorists think same-sex marriage will make their job easier, they are mistaken. I don't think the American public will have much trouble distinguishing the principle of same-sex marriage (one for everybody—the principle of monogamy itself) from the principle of traditional polygamy (many for some, none for others), or the principle of postmodern polyamory (everyone for everyone), or the principle of incestuous marriage (anyone for everyone), or any other principle. If anything, same-sex marriage would heighten the contrast. Polygamists would find themselves arguing for plural marriage at a time when the country had just confirmed the one-person-one-spouse rule in the most dramatic possible way.

Same-sex marriage is not, as so often alleged, a slippery slope to polygamy or anything else. Just the opposite: it is a natural stopping place. In fact, it is *the* natural stopping place. It is the bottom of the slope. When everybody can marry one other person, there will be no one else left to take in. Polygamists and polyamorists and incestuists and the others will be left pushing their boulders not down from an outcropping but up from a canyon.

8

Men Behaving Badly

Not long ago, on a talk-radio program out of Charlotte, North Carolina, I debated a Baptist minister named Joseph Chambers about gay marriage. For most of the hour, things went pretty much as expected, but in the last few minutes I got a nasty jolt. A listener called in to name all the diseases spread by gay sex. I replied that gay marriage is the solution, not the problem. Give people a home and a spouse and a marital sex life, and they are probably not out on the streets spreading germs. If marriage were banned for heterosexuals and steady relationships were discouraged and even prosecuted, imagine the promiscuity and disease (and sleaze and misery) that would result. I told the caller she might as well say that, because the world is full of dangerous infections, antibiotics should be banned. It was at that moment, just when I was feeling pretty clever, that Rev. Chambers shot me this challenge (I'll paraphrase, but closely): "I want to ask you a question. Can you say that you have been 100 percent faithful to your partner?"

That flustered me. Since time immemorial, if there is one question which civilized people expect never to be asked in public, it is, "Have you cheated on your spouse?" In olden times that

question would get you challenged to a duel and maybe killed;
even today, a punch in the nose is a fairly appropriate answer. A
mean drunk might ask such a question at a party, but he could
count on never being invited back. A question like that could
wreck a marriage. Many is the marriage which is preserved by
one spouse's quietly tolerating what the other gets up to. One of
the most important ways society supports matrimony is by looking away from adultery as long as the cheater keeps the philan-
dering out of sight and the cuckolded partner chooses not to blow
the whistle.

But here I was, being asked point-blank, in the hearing of most
of North Carolina, if I had ever cheated on my other half. And I'm
not even married! I *can't* be married! I had nothing to be ashamed
of, but I deeply resented the question. So I said what Gary Hart,
the Democratic presidential candidate, said in 1987 when a
Washington Post reporter set a new low for political journalism by
asking, at a press conference, "Have you ever committed adultery?" Hart replied, "I do not have to answer that." (He was right.
So was his wife, Lee, who said, "In all honesty, if it doesn't bother
me, I don't think it ought to bother anyone else.") When I refused
to answer the question, Rev. Chambers claimed the kill. "You've
just told me all I need to know."

I was angry. Rev. Chambers, I was sure, would never have
asked a heterosexual interlocutor, on live radio, if he had ever
cheated on his wife and then accused him of adultery if he
sought to protect his privacy. An outrageous double standard!
Once I cooled down, however, I partially changed my mind. To
many Americans, homosexual marriage and, for that matter,
homosexuality itself are terra incognita. As heterosexuals grapple
with gay marriage, they are going to want answers to a lot of questions, including some they have no business asking. One is the
generalized form of the question Rev. Chambers asked me: Will
married gay men be rampant adulterers?

———

So far in this book I have made a critical assumption: that marriage will change homosexual culture more than homosexual culture will change marriage. Critics of same-sex marriage justifiably call me to account on that point. Their answer to Barney Frank's challenge—how would my being able to marry harm your marriage?—goes something like this:

"Maybe your marriage wouldn't hurt mine. And we have nothing against you or homosexuals or even, necessarily, against homosexuality as such. But it is our duty and yours to face facts, and among those facts is that men are different from women where sex is concerned. They are more interested in sexual variety and so more prone to promiscuity. It is not just marriage which civilizes men, it is women, because women demand fidelity. Left to their own devices, men are quite casual about sleeping around. Some of them sleep around a lot. If you want a demonstration, just look at gay-male culture, with its obsession with sex and its toleration—sometimes glorification—of promiscuity. And it is a fact that a relatively high proportion of gay-male couples are 'open' to sex outside the relationship.

"Marriage between men and women relies on the norm of fidelity, of exclusivity: of a promise made to one and no other, a promise socially acknowledged on that basis. Gay men will disregard this norm. They will be nonchalant about adultery. Many of them will have 'open' marriages, taking (or sharing) multiple outside sex partners. In other words, they will be married without acting married. Their example will lead to a general devaluing of faithfulness. Adultery will become part of the marital landscape. It will be harder to tell children that adultery is wrong. With the stigma eroded, more straight husbands will be unfaithful and more marriages will break up, the last thing marriage needs right now.

"Given the nature of men, the question is not whether male-male couples will change marriage, or in which direction. The only question is how much damage they will do. Introducing same-sex marriage at a time when the institution's condition is already shaky enough is a risk no responsible policy maker should want to take."

On its face, a powerful argument. To approach it, I'll divide it into its three essential constituent parts, claims of three distinct types:

1. *Empirical:* "Men are different from women, and male-male couples are inherently more prone to adultery."
2. *Predictive:* "Gay couples' infidelity will prove contagious. Their adultery will damage or destroy the norm of fidelity among straight couples."
3. *Prescriptive:* "Therefore the best policy is to keep same-sex marriage illegal."

My view is that Claim 1 is probably true but easily and often exaggerated. Claim 2 is false. Claim 3 is also false. I believe gay marriage will do much more to strengthen the norm of marriage than it will do to weaken the norm of fidelity—and indeed I doubt it will, on balance, weaken the norm of fidelity at all. Especially in comparison with the alternatives, gay marriage is part of the solution, after all.

———

In the summer of 2003, on his way to do other things, a law professor at the University of California at Los Angeles named Eugene Volokh—he is straight, by the way—started poking into the conventional wisdom that homosexual men are wildly promiscuous. What he found surprised him. Every time he looked at a study cited in support of what he came to regard as the myth of wild gay promiscuity, it fell apart.

One 1992 book, for instance, reported that the median homosexual male had more than 250 sexual partners. When Volokh tracked down the study cited, it turned out to be limited to the San Francisco Bay Area—in 1970! As if that were not enough, in recruiting their interviewees the study's authors had relied heavily on bars, bathhouses (sex clubs), and public sex-cruising spots. They had also, among other methods, taken out ads, which, in 1970, were hardly likely to elicit responses from private, stay-at-home homosexuals. The researchers had duly cautioned that their sample was "non-representative," a caveat which subsequent citations had not seen fit to emphasize. In another book, this one from 1993, the author cited studies "showing 'homosexual men . . . reported a median of 1,160 lifetime sexual partners.'" Wow. When Volokh looked up that reference, he discovered that two words had been omitted from the quotation and replaced with an ellipsis: "with AIDS." Throughout the section, he found, research that was cited as evidence of gay-male promiscuity turned out to be studies of men who were mostly or entirely drawn from samples of patients with sexually transmitted diseases. In other words, the cited studies, as Volokh commented in his Web log, *The Volokh Conspiracy,* "were focused not on homosexual men generally, but only on a sample that would predictably have many more sexual partners than the average gay man." Promiscuity, after all, increases the risk of getting HIV.

Intrigued, he kept digging. "The only halfway reliable data on these sorts of issues would come from random samples of the population at large," Volokh wrote, "and of course it's hard to get data about homosexuals from those samples, since they're such a small fraction of the population—it would take a huge study to get any sort of statistically significant information." The research he was able to find, however, was consistent. Most gay men have had more sex partners than most straight men, but the difference is nothing like the multiples of 20 and 100 which are sometimes claimed. One broad study (Laumann, Gagnon, Michael, and Michaels, *The Social Organization of Sexuality: Sexual Practices in the United States,* which surveyed Americans between eighteen and fifty-nine years of age in the early 1990s) found that straight women had averaged about five partners since the age of eighteen, compared with about seventeen for straight men and twenty-seven or so for gay men (give or take a dozen, which means there is a lot of noise in the gay-male numbers). Straight women reported having, on average, just one partner in the previous year, straight men closer to two, and gay men around three.

Another analysis, drawn from the General Social Survey data set, found very similar averages, but also showed medians. That information is valuable, because medians may better reflect what the typical person is doing. (The *median* is the level which half the population is above and half is below. An *average* can be skewed by a few unusual individuals at the extreme high end. The average income of any twenty ordinary people plus Bill Gates would be millions of dollars, but the median would be more like $40,000.) It turned out that the median straight female reported having had three sex partners since age eighteen, the median straight male six, and the median gay male ten. Volokh concluded:

> Now it does appear that a significant minority of American gay males do have lots of sexual partners. Moreover, the median American gay male does have somewhat more sexual partners than the median straight male (likely ten to twenty lifetime partners for gays as opposed to five to ten for straights . . .).
>
> But the claim that the median American gay male (not just a minority of gays) is hyper-promiscuous (not just a bit more promiscuous than heterosexuals) appears to be false.

"Is Promiscuity Innate?" asked the *Washington Post* in a 2003 headline. The article reported on a study of 16,000 people on every inhabited continent. The finding: "Men everywhere—whether single, married, or gay—want more sexual partners than women do." Aha! Men are tomcats! But read on:

> Asked how many partners they desired over the next month, men on average said 1.87, while women said 0.78. Men said that over the next ten years they wanted 5.95 partners, while women said they wanted 2.17.

More than a quarter of heterosexual men wanted more than one partner in the next month, as did 29.1 percent of gay men and 30.1 percent of bisexual men, the study said. Just 4.4 percent of heterosexual women, 5.5 percent of lesbians, and 15.6 percent of bisexual women sought more than one partner.

In other words: men want almost three times more sex partners over the course of ten years than women do, but the number is still fewer than six partners. About 70 percent of men, whether gay, straight, or bi, agree with the even larger majority of women that one partner in the next month is enough.

My own hunch is that men evolved with an urge to spread their seed, but they also evolved with a longing for the comfort of a mate and a family and a baby they could be reasonably confident is their own. After a while, the sex gets old and men look for love, and to get love means giving emotionally: forming stable ties and reciprocally putting one person ahead of all others. Women probably settle down more readily than men ("Q: What does a lesbian bring to her second date? A: A moving van"), but the two sexes overlap more than they differ. Not for nothing is the lusty young lass a stock figure of folklore.

This fairly unsensational view of things certainly comports with my own knowledge of gay life. At the extremes, some gay men and lesbians live on different planets ("Q: What does a gay man bring to his second date? A: What second date?"), but most people live life toward the center, where differences are much less pronounced. Without the restraining influence of women, most gay men get on with their lives in an unremarkable way. In fact, many single gay men seem to spend half their time complaining that, as the song goes, they can't get no satisfaction. Some men do go wild, although they usually get over it. While they are being wild, they can dive in over their heads, no doubt about it. I once wrote an article about a troubled young gay man who had compulsive unprotected sex until he got HIV. (*Then* he got his life together.) But these men are busy frequenting circuit parties and dance clubs. They are not the likely candidates for marriage, any more than the wildest and youngest straight men are. They will be the last to be touched by the culture of marriage and the last to touch it.

———————

All of this is by way of warning against getting carried away with the rather Victorian notion that men are beasts who must be tamed by chaste damsels. However, it is still possible to press a subtler point. "Men have a more relaxed attitude about adultery than women do. So gay-male couples are more open to outside sex."

I think this is true—up to a point. But the point is not where some critics of same-sex marriage think it is. Men do seem to have an easier time than women detaching sex from love and regarding it as a purely physical outlet. (Which is why the prostitution and pornography industries serve a predominantly male clientele.) The result is that, in my experience, male-male couples are less likely than male-female couples to regard adultery as a deal breaker.

That is a far cry, however, from saying that male-male couples are indifferent to adultery. I know many monogamous gay-male couples. It wouldn't surprise me to learn that they are more likely, on average, to slip up than straight couples are, although I have no way of knowing. (Adultery, after all, is hardly unknown in the straight world; more than 20 percent of husbands report having cheated on their wives, and those are just the ones who admit to it.) But adultery is not part of the deal; it is a transgression, a violation of trust. The couple's ability to cope and move on should not, I think, be held against them.

As for nonmonogamous gay couples, the ones I know of tend to fall into two categories. The first consists of people who aren't strongly committed and are still shopping around or trying out the relationship: people who do not consider themselves to be in anything like a marriage. (In gay relationships, remember, boundaries can be unclear, because marriage is illegal.) Among this contingent, a particularly common reason for breaking up is that one partner is ready to move to monogamy and the other is not. Such couples are not so much nonmonogamous as they are pre-monogamous (or just not interested in settling down).

The real concern, presumably, is with gay couples who build in a certain tolerance for sleeping around as part of the deal. That sort of arrangement is rare among committed heterosexual couples (although I personally know of one), but not uncommon among gay men. Note, however, what this is not: an "open" relationship in which both partners take an orgiastic, no-worries attitude to outside sex. Few same-sex relationships—serious ones, defined by long-term commitment—could survive with both parties spending a lot of nights in other people's beds, and gay partners, not being idiots or naïfs, know it. The usual attitude among this sub-category of couples is: "Now and then is okay, but regularly or often is definitely not okay." So adultery—some adultery—is regarded as a fact of life. Sometimes both partake, but often one member of the couple accommodates the other's adventuring, provided it isn't too frequent.

If you think about it, this is not so unlike the quiet practice of some straight couples. Bill and Hillary Clinton may have had such an arrangement, at least for a time. François Mitterrand, the late French president, kept a mistress for much of his married life, and had a child by her. She came to his funeral, where she grieved together with his wife. Mme Mitterrand later said, "Yes, I had married a seducer, and I had to put up with that. I was never bored with him." Such unions are not closed but also not quite open. Call them ajar.

None of this is to defend the morality of adultery. It is merely to introduce a note of realism. I think it is almost certainly true that male-male couples put a somewhat lower value on sexual fidelity within a relationship than do male-female couples—on average. But how big is the "somewhat"? I doubt the more extreme guesses. I think it will be a wide spectrum, but the average difference will prove unstartling, and I think the gap will narrow, in favor of fidelity, over time. Today's gay-male couples are the baseline. The direction from here is up.

One reason I'm optimistic is this: if today's male-male couples take sexual exclusivity less seriously than do male-female couples, that is partly because they are male-male, but it is also partly—perhaps very largely—because *not a single one of them is married.* Not a single one of them has ever been married. Not a single one of them can expect to marry. Even if all of them were perfectly faithful all the time, they *still* would not be able to marry. Their culture has only just crawled out from the Long Dark Age into a tenuous respectability, after having been condemned for generations to a sexual underground of one-night or ten-minute stands with strangers. And these are the conditions under which we must decide whether male couples can be fit for marriage? The reason we know they will never act married is that, after centuries of alienation from even the barest hope of marriage, they do not *already* act married?

In 2003, the *Washington Times,* a conservative newspaper, published an article headlined: "Study Finds Gay Unions Brief." It went on to quote Dutch research which found that "homosexual relationships" last a year and a half on average. By way of comparison, it then noted that 67 percent of American first marriages last ten years. So "relationships" are less durable than marriages? Stop the presses! It is an established fact that even serious cohabitations are short-lived compared with marriages, and, of course, the term "relationships" refers not only to serious cohabitation but to short-term dating. If you compared heterosexual marriages with "heterosexual relationships," you would find the latter to be a great deal less durable. The same article went on to note that earlier studies "indicated that homosexual men are not monogamous, even when they are involved in long-term relationships." The statement is true only if you change it to read, "Homosexual men are not *as* monogamous, even when they are involved in long-term relationships," but hold on. Not one of those "relationships" is a marriage. Nonmarital relationships are less likely to be monogamous: this is news? I would have called it a pretty well-known fact, and I would have thought it one of the better reasons for marriage, including gay marriage.

The debate, at bottom, is about an empirical question on which we have little or no data. On the one hand, male-male married couples may well be less strictly monogamous—on average—than male-female married couples. On the other hand, male-male married couples are likely to be more strictly monogamous—on average—than male-male unmarried couples; and tradition-minded male couples will be the most likely to marry. Given the surprising speed and grace with which male-male unmarried couples are already settling down, I think it is pretty much a certainty that, once gay couples are equipped with the entitlements and entanglements of legal marriage, same-sex relationships will continue to move toward both durability and exclusivity.

Would male-male couples ever completely close the gaps with male-female couples? The durability gap, quite possibly. The exclusivity gap? I doubt it. Narrower, yes. Closed, no. The dynamics of a male-male union will never be—on average—quite the same as the dynamics of an opposite-sex union. (For that matter, female-female unions will have their own patterns, too.) Nonetheless, the social benefits of more stable, more committed same-sex relationships are still worth having, even if (on average) the exclusivity gap doesn't close all the way. But that conclusion only brings us to Claim 2 of "men behaving badly": to whatever extent male-male couples are more adulterous, will they influence male-female couples in the same direction?

———

Norms are important. That is why it matters so much to shore up marriage's status as *the* norm for serious relationships, straight or

gay. As regulators of human behavior, norms are at least as powerful as laws and infinitely subtler. By the same token, understanding them can be tricky. It is entirely possible that two things could
happen at once. Same-sex marriage could strengthen the norm of
marriage (good, in my opinion) while weakening the norm of
fidelity within marriage (bad, in my opinion). Any honest assessment needs to consider both sides of the equation.

To clarify the discussion, and for the purposes of argument
only, let me stipulate something I absolutely do not believe.
Assume that marriage would have little or no effect on the sexual
behavior of gay-male couples. In other words, assume that married male couples would act pretty much as unmarried male
couples do today. Some married male couples would be monogamous. Some male couples would remain unmarried. But some
unknown but potentially large share of married gay-male couples
would be, to one extent or another, nonmonogamous. What
would be the effect?

Norms are what respectable people regard as respectable
behavior. We learn them from our parents, our teachers, our religious traditions, our laws; not least, however, we learn them from
the example of others. Divorce was once rare and stigmatized; now
it is common and normal. Although part of the change stemmed
from legal reforms that made divorce easier to get, much of the
change resulted from the power of example. When more respectable people began divorcing, divorce became more respectable.
Adultery has to some extent gone the other way. In my grand-
father's day, many high-status men had mistresses, and many
medium-status and low-status men had flings or paid occasional
visits to houses of ill repute, particularly when they were drunk or
on the road (where would the traveling-salesman joke be otherwise?). Such behavior was not respectable, but many women
accepted it—they had no choice—and if some corporate tycoon
was known to make special demands on his secretaries, polite
society mostly looked the other way (it had no choice, either).

When economic independence and available divorce gave women an out, however, they were able to walk away from a philanderer. Polite society became less tolerant of that stock figure of novels and soap operas, the cad.

The minor point I want to make is that, to some extent, the norms of fidelity and durability may work at cross-purposes. About the time prostitution faded as a middle-class institution, the divorce rate began to rise. In Japan today, marriages are much more stable than in the United States, and the divorce rate is much lower; going to Japan is like visiting America in the 1950s, in that respect—and also in another. Corporate and political honchos frequently engage in what used to be called mashing; married salarymen are well known throughout Asia for letting their hair (read: pants) down on trips abroad; "hostess bars" cater to husbands who want more sexual attention or variety than they get at home; the prostitution trade thrives on middle-class custom, as it once did in America. So it was, anyway, when I lived in Japan in 1990, and although American-style mores are creeping in, I doubt things have changed all that much.

Here is something that American social conservatives are understandably reluctant to think about: What if, twenty years after gay marriage became legal, male-male spouses had higher adultery rates but lower divorce rates than male-female spouses? I'm not predicting it would happen; I'm just making the point that one should not simply assume that more adultery means more divorce. If gay men tolerated more extramarital sex but stayed together longer, their example would not be entirely bad.

On the other hand, male couples might have more extramarital sex *and* higher divorce rates. After all, fewer of them will have children to stay together for, and they will all be men. So on to the major point.

Adultery may once have been widely winked at in America, but it was not normal. Like homosexuality, it was generally tolerated, but only on the condition that it stay in the closet. The official rule was: "No adultery, ever." But the unofficial rule was, "If it happens, make sure it stays out of sight." If a cheating husband, paramour in tow, kept his end of the bargain by checking into a motel on the far end of town as "Mr. and Mrs. John Doe," no one asked questions. Blowing the whistle was up to the wife. Adulterers didn't tell, and no one else asked.

But woe unto the man who flouted the rules by flaunting his mistress. If he showed up at the office holiday party with her, his employer would find reasons not to promote him, his church or club would turn its back on him, he would be told he had become too controversial for a career in public life or even to be a Scout master. Norms are set by what we do openly, in public: by what is respectable to acknowledge and talk about in front of children.

Hidden in the "men behaving badly" argument is the assumption that male-male unions will not only be adulterous but *openly* adulterous. If gay spouses kept their adultery secret, after all, it could hardly become a bad example to others. But the hidden assumption is far-fetched. Gay-male spouses will value respectability. They will have parents and in-laws and other family members whom they will not want to disappoint. It would hardly be in their interest to advertise that their marriage is not serious. I can imagine a handful of gay radicals boasting of their "open" marriages in polite society ("Hi, I'm Tom, and this is my husband, Brian, and we both sleep around"). But they will be far from the norm. Candid discussions of sexual exclusivity will be for intimate friends, most of them gay. That is, in fact, already the case. If you are straight and know a committed gay couple, do you know whether they sleep around? Do you want or need to know? Do they want or need to tell you? "I'm an adulterer" is not a message civil people, gay or straight, put on their car bumper. I suppose gay husbands might be less secretive about their affairs than straight husbands, if only because they might not be as worried about hiding their behavior from their spouse (women care more—on average). That said, the difference will be slight. For its part, straight America will, or at least should, do its part by not asking nosey questions. Whatever goes on inside a marriage—gay or straight—is no one else's business, as long as the marriage works. Most gay adultery will thus be invisible to the world at large, as it already is, and as straight adultery is.

So now some arithmetic. According to the 2000 census, the United States has about 55 million married couples. Assume that same-sex marriage were legalized tomorrow. The census counts about 600,000 same-sex, unmarried-partner households; assume they all got married. (The 600,000 figure is almost certainly an undercount, given the difficulty of tracking down the relatively small numbers of people involved and the reluctance of some gay couples to declare themselves to strangers from the government. But it is probably a reasonably good proxy for the number of same-sex couples who might come forward to be married in the near future, because some uncounted couples would want to marry and some counted couples would not.) Of those same-sex couples, half, or about 300,000, are lesbian. Since no one accuses them of being incorrigible adulterers, we can focus on the 300,000 male-male couples. Of those, figure, I think conservatively, that only a third are monogamous (we don't really know, so that is just a guess for purposes of discussion). That would leave 200,000 gay-male couples who would be to some degree adulterous. Of those, however, only a fraction would be public about their adultery: maybe 5 percent, maybe 20 percent (although I doubt it); for argument's sake, figure 10 percent. Grand totals: over 55 million married couples in America—and 20,000 of them, or not quite 0.04 percent, visibly adulterous male couples. Indeed, openly adulterous couples would make up only 3 percent of *gay* marriages.

You can use different assumptions to get different numbers. You can assume that 5 percent of the population is gay, that gay-marriage rates would equal straight-marriage rates (implying not quite 3 million same-sex married couples), that two-thirds of those couples would be male (about 1.8 million), that three-fourths of the male couples would be nonmonogamous (about 1.4 million), and that fully half of the nonmonogamous male couples would trumpet their marriage's openness. Those are the most liberal assumptions which I think might be remotely plausible, and they still add up to fewer than 700,000 openly adulterous gay marriages, or 1.25 percent of all marriages, and only a quarter of *gay* marriages.

We are asked to believe, then, that a small subset of same-sex marriages—the fringe of a fringe—will set the marital pattern for the rest of the United States. We might as well regard nudists as the trendsetters for fashion. It seems more likely that the few will pattern their relationships on the many than the other way around. Openly adulterous male-male couples will be little more than cultural curiosities, like hippies or Scientologists. Even most gay people will consider them odd.

Moreover, even if same-sex marriage were legalized, heterosexual marriages *would still have women in them.* If it is the case, as we are so often told, that women are biologically different from men in their lower interest in and toleration of infidelity, they will continue to be a restraining influence on their male partners. The only way to make sense of the claim that male-male adultery would spread to male-female couples is to assume that maleness itself would spread to millions of American women.

So the theory that same-sex marriage would lead to a plague of adultery in straight marriages defies not only arithmetic but biology. Yes, gays have cultural influence and visibility, but for every married gay couple who flaunt their adultery, there will be many others who flaunt their commitment. When a prominent actor receives his Oscar by thanking his loyal husband of twenty years, while the camera cuts to the husband glowing with pride and choking back tears, that will be the kind of advertisement for marriage which money can't buy.

And if I'm wrong? What if gay men were indeed flagrantly bad marital citizens and straight couples were influenced by their example? Should same-sex marriage then be illegal? To answer yes would be both unwise and unfair.

Sustaining a committed, faithful relationship may be more of a challenge for gay-male couples. Surely, however, the right response is to give gay partners support and help in meeting the challenge, rather than telling them not to bother trying. Conservatives, of all people, ought to understand this. Try to imagine them saying: "Young men in the inner cities are prone to promiscuity and infidelity. Many of them don't fully understand or accept the obligations of marriage. Some of them glamorize promiscuity and sexual prowess. Some of them know only a culture in which marriage seems a faraway prospect, almost unreal. If they get married, a large share will cheat, and many will end up divorced or separated. Plus they are trendsetters. Through popular culture they will set a bad example for middle-class couples. So they ought to be prohibited from marrying. In fact, even if some of them managed to form committed, devoted unions and to accept the burdens of marriage, the law should tell them they can only be shacked up. The law should signal that *nothing* they do by way of commitment would be enough to get them all the way to marriage. This may not be a policy inner-city men will like. But it's the price we pay to defend marriage from their culture."

Obviously, no conservative says anything like that. Instead, and to their credit, promarriage conservatives have taken the lead in advocating public and private programs that promote and support marriage among the welfare population. In every context except the gay one, people readily see that stopping marriage is not the right way to stop infidelity. Instead, they look to community groups, religious organizations, social-service providers, private counselors, and even welfare caseworkers to help newcomers find their way in the culture of marriage. In every context except the gay one, society understands that the message to send is: "First, get married.

Tie the knot. Then we have something to work with. It may not be perfect, but it beats the alternative." In every context except the gay one, society understands that the norms of durability (sticking with the marriage) and of exclusivity (sticking with one's spouse) are important, but that the norm of marriage itself is what matters the most—hands down.

Questions for married readers. Remember that two-day, four-part Marital Aptitude Test you were required to pass before you were allowed to get your license? Remember when the social worker visited your home and interviewed your neighbors to make sure you were faithful enough to your partner to qualify for marriage? Remember how, before they issued your license, the authorities looked up your age group and ethnic group and religious group to check that the odds of your staying married were up to par? No? You mean they just let you go down to City Hall, pay a fee, and get a marriage license—just like that? What kind of crazy country would allow that?

Only the kind of crazy country which recognizes that, as with so many of life's basic responsibilities (employment, parenthood, voting), the only way to learn is by doing—so the way to become good at being married is by being married. No two marriages are alike. Each is self-generative, within a framework of norms and prerogatives supplied by law and community. You can do some things to prepare for marriage (although cohabiting appears not to be one of them: for reasons as yet unclear, married couples are *less* likely to endure if they live together first). But, in fact, nothing can prepare you for the new social and legal responsibilities you bear the first morning you wake up married, and for the new way your family and friends and partner (now spouse) look at you.

For me, the fidelity double standard—the insistence that gay people become model marital citizens *before* they can have the right to marry—is the bitterest of all the ironies in the gay-marriage debate, and also the most twisted. Applying a fertility standard only to homosexuals, never to heterosexuals, is inconsistent, but at least it is true that all same-sex couples are infertile. Critics who harp on gay infidelity, however, are playing the odds. They treat gay people not as individuals but as averages. It is not possible for a gay couple to conceive children, but it is certainly possible for them to stay faithful to each other, and many do, just as many straight couples do not. Even if all gay-male couples were adulterous, their number would not approach that of adulterous heterosexual husbands. But all such considerations are deemed inconsequential, because the gay *average* is below par. One wonders: Exactly what proportion of gay men would need to be faithful in order to earn homosexuals the legal right to marry? Seventy-five to 80 percent—the male heterosexual average, if you trust surveys? Ninety percent? And how many heterosexuals would agree that their own legal right to marry should depend on the average fidelity of other heterosexuals?

In how many ways, then, is the "men behaving badly" argument unfair? It taxes homosexual couples with not living up to the rules of a club they are forbidden to join. It obsesses about the bad example some gay spouses may set, while giving no weight to the good example which would surely be set by others. It assumes that any increase, however small, in the heterosexual divorce rate would be unacceptable, but that shutting out homosexuals from the benefits of marriage is just fine. It tells gays they won't be good marital citizens and then denies them any opportunity to prove the claim wrong. It applies to all homosexuals a fidelity test which applies to *no* heterosexuals. And then, having established a fidelity test for gays, it throws away the results.

Throws away the results? Just so. The strongest case you could make for denying marriage to all gay couples because of the average rate of gay infidelity is that sorting the likely faithful from the likely unfaithful couples isn't practical. Someone might say, "Fidelity-testing couples would be hopelessly inaccurate and intrusive even if it were doable, which it isn't. But one thing we do know is that gay men are less sexually exclusive, and it's irresponsible not to act on that knowledge. As a proxy for infidelity, homosexuality will just have to do."

The problem, of course, is this: lesbians. As far as I know, no one even bothers to contend that lesbian unions are more infidelity-prone than straight ones. If anything, they seem to be more exclusive. If "men behaving badly" proponents were serious about protecting marriage from infidelity rather than from homosexuals, they would welcome lesbian couples with open arms. "Here's a group with a great average!" they would say. "Come join us! Come share your good example!"

Well, they do not say that. Usually they say nothing. During the entire same-sex-marriage debate, I can think of only a single instance in which anybody even tried to justify the lesbian exclusion, and that justification would have to be described as desperate. In August 2003, in *The Weekly Standard,* Stanley Kurtz argued that lesbian couples who bear children with sperm donors sometimes set up de facto three-parent families with the natural father, who is close to the couple but not sexually involved. "Once lesbian couples can marry, there will be a powerful legal case for extending parental recognition to triumvirates." And "legally recognized triple parenting will eventually usher in state-sanctioned triple (and therefore group) marriage."

This, of course, is an argument about parental rights, not marriage. It has no bearing at all on lesbian couples without children. And it is a classic in the genre of inventing homosexual horror stories about arrangements which, in a heterosexual context, are quite routine. An unmarried man and woman have a baby. The woman gets custody and then marries another man. The child now has a stepfather. But the mother still wants her child to know his natural dad. Dad gets involved in family life and has certain legal rights. Uh-oh! Looks like "legally recognized triple parenting." Triple marriages must be just around the corner!

With that one eccentric exception, gay-marriage opponents simply avoid the subject of lesbians. When the issue is pressed, they dismiss it as a debater's point or, more often, they just ignore it and keep harping on gay men. What average level of sexual restraint, then, would earn homosexuals the right to marry? Judging from the insistence on excluding lesbians, apparently not even a level that meets or exceeds the heterosexual standard would suffice for homosexuals. In other words, once again we seem to have been wasting our time. The problem is not gay promiscuity or adultery. It is gay love and commitment.

9

The Debt to Tradition

B ut it is *marriage* we are talking about.

Some readers of this book have been for gay marriage all along. Some have been against it and could not be budged by anything I might say. Some may have started out feeling one way and changed their minds (I won't ask in which direction). And some are members of another group, probably a large one—people of goodwill toward homosexuals, people who pride themselves on thinking for themselves and caring about their fellow citizens. Some may agree with me that there are plausible, even compelling, reasons to prefer same-sex marriage to the alternatives, and that many of the objections are overwrought, unfair, or misguided. And yet these readers hesitate, draw back. They have reservations which are hard to pin down but which seem not a whit less powerful for that. They may cite religion or culture, but the roots of their misgivings go even deeper. Press them, and they might say something like this:

"I understand how hard it must be to live a marriageless life, or at least I try to understand. I see that some of the objections to same-sex marriage are more about excluding gays than defending marriage. Believe me, I am no homophobe; I want gay people to have joy and comfort. I respect their relationships and their love, even if they are not what I would want for myself. But look. No matter how I come at this question, I keep bumping into the same wall. For the entire history of civilization, marriage has been between men and women. In every religion, every culture, every society—maybe with some minor and rare exceptions, none of them part of our own heritage—marriage has been reserved for the union of male and female. All the words in the world cannot change that. Same-sex marriage would not be an incremental tweak but a radical reform, a break with all of Western history. I'm sorry. I am not prepared to take that step, not when we are talking about civilization's bedrock institution. I don't know that I can even give you good reasons. It is just that what you are asking for is too much."

Sometimes the simple arguments are deeper than the clever ones; the argument from tradition is just such a case. Instead of entangling itself in complicated distinctions and rationalizations (and then applying them inconsistently to reach an antigay result), it is woven of a plain-spun social wisdom. There are really only two objections to same-sex marriage which are intellectually honest and internally consistent. One is the simple antigay position: "It is the law's job to stigmatize and disadvantage homosexuals, and the marriage ban is a means to that end." The other is the argument from tradition—which turns out, on inspection, not to be so simple. Perhaps it doesn't matter what marriage is for, or perhaps we can't know exactly what marriage is for. Perhaps it is enough simply to say that marriage is as it is, and you can't just make it something else. I call this the Hayekian argument, for F. A. Hayek, one of the twentieth century's great economists and philosophers.

––––––––––

Friedrich August von Hayek (1899–1992), Austrian by birth, British by adoption, winner of the 1974 Nobel Prize in economics, is generally known as one of the leading theoreticians of free-market economics and, more broadly, of libertarian (he always said liberal) social thought. He was eloquent in his defense of the dynamic change that markets bring, but many people are less aware of a deeply traditionalist, conservative strand in his thinking, a strand that traces its lineage back at least to Edmund Burke, the eighteenth-century English philosopher and politician. Burke, famously, poured scorn on the French Revolution and its claims to be inventing a new and enlightened social order. The attempt to reinvent society on abstract principles would result not in utopia, he contended, but in tyranny. For Burke, the existing order might be flawed, even in some respects evil, but it had an organic sense to it, and so throwing the whole system out the window would bring greater flaws and larger evils.

Outside Britain and America, few people listened. The French Revolution inspired generations of reformers to propose their own utopian social experiments. Communism was one such, fascism another; today, radical Islamism (the political philosophy, not the religion) is yet one more. "The attempt to make heaven on earth invariably produces hell," wrote Karl Popper, another great Austrian-British philosopher, in 1945, when the totalitarian night looked darkest. He and Hayek came of age in the same intellectual climate, when not only Marxists and fascists but many mainstream Western intellectuals took for granted that a handful of smart people could make better social decisions than could chaotic markets, blind traditions, or crude majorities.

It was in opposition to, as he called it, this "fatal conceit" that Hayek organized much of his career. He vigorously argued the case for the dynamism and "spontaneous order" of free markets, but he asserted just as vigorously that the dynamism and freedom of constant change were possible only within a restraining framework of rules and customs and institutions which, for the most part, do not change, or change at a speed they themselves set. No expert or political leader can possibly have enough knowledge to get up every morning and order the world from scratch: decide whether to wear clothing, which side of the street to drive on, what counts as mine and what as yours. "Every man growing up in a given culture will find in himself rules, or may discover that he acts in accordance with rules—and will similarly recognize the actions of others as conforming or not conforming to various rules," Hayek wrote in his 1973 book *Law, Legislation, and Liberty*. The rules, he added, are not necessarily innate or unchangeable, but "they are part of a cultural heritage which is likely to be fairly constant, especially so long as they are not articulated in words and therefore also are not discussed or consciously examined."

Hayek the economist is famous for the insight that, in a market system, the prices generated by impersonal forces may not make sense from any one person's point of view, but they encode far more economic information than even the cleverest person or the most powerful computer could ever hope to organize. In a similar fashion, Hayek the social philosopher wrote that human societies' complicated web of culture, traditions, and institutions embodies far more cultural knowledge than any one person could master. Like prices, the customs generated by societies over time may seem irrational or arbitrary. But the very fact that these customs have evolved and survived to come down to us implies that a practical logic may be embedded in them which might not be apparent from even a sophisticated analysis. And the web of custom cannot be torn apart and reordered at will, because once its internal logic is violated it may fall apart.

It was on this point that Hayek was particularly outspoken. Intellectuals and visionaries who seek to deconstruct and rationally rebuild social traditions will produce not a better order but chaos. In his 1952 work *The Counter-Revolution of Science: Studies in the Abuse of Reason,* Hayek made a statement which demands to be quoted in full and read at least twice:

It may indeed prove to be far the most difficult and not the least important task for human reason rationally to comprehend its own limitations. It is essential for the growth of reason that as individuals we should bow to forces and obey principles which we cannot hope fully to understand, yet on which the advance and even the preservation of civilization depends. Historically this has been achieved by the influence of the various religious creeds and by traditions and superstitions which made man submit to those forces by an appeal to his emotions rather than to his reason. The most dangerous stage in the growth of civilization may well be that in which man has come to regard all these beliefs as superstitions and refuses to accept or to submit to anything which he does not rationally understand. The rationalist whose reason is not sufficient to teach him those limitations of the powers of conscious reason, and who despises all the institutions and customs which have not been consciously designed, would thus become the destroyer of the civilization built upon them. This may well prove a hurdle which man will repeatedly reach, only to be thrown back into barbarism.

For secular intellectuals who are unhappy with the evolved framework of marriage and who are excluded from it—in other words, for people like me—the Hayekian argument is very challenging. The age-old stigmas attached to illegitimacy and out-of-wedlock pregnancy were crude and unfair to women and children. On the male side, shotgun marriages were coercive and intrusive and often made poor matches. The shame associated with divorce seemed to make no sense at all. But when modern societies abolished the stigmas on illegitimacy, divorce, and all the rest, whole portions of the social structure just caved in.

Not long ago I had dinner with a friend who is a devout Christian. He has a heart of gold, knows and likes gay people, and has warmed to the idea of civil unions. But when I asked him about gay marriage, he replied with a firm no. I asked if he imagined there was anything I could say that might budge him. He thought for a moment and then said no again. Why? Because, he said, male-female marriage is a sacrament from God. It predates the

Constitution and every other law of man. We could not, in that sense, change it even if we wanted to. I asked if it might alter his conclusion to reflect that legal marriage is a secular institution, that the separation of church and state requires us to distinguish God's law from civil law, and that we must refrain from using law to impose one group's religious precepts on the rest of society. He shook his head. No, he said. This is bigger than that.

I felt he had not answered my argument. His God is not mine, and in a secular country, law can and should be influenced by religious teachings but must not enforce them. Yet really it was I who had not answered his argument, in some deeper way. Precisely because legal marriage is a secular institution, I have had little to say in this book about the role of religion in validating marriage. To many readers, that must seem odd. After all, the majority of people who marry do so in a religious ceremony. It is a cleric who administers the vows, usually in a place of worship. "Dearly beloved, we are gathered here in the sight of God, and in the face of this company," begins the ceremony: although civil society must be present, God gets top billing. For many people, God creates a marriage which the government merely acknowledges. No doubt the government has the right to set the law of marriage without kowtowing to the Vatican (for example). But that does not make it wise for the government to disregard the centuries of tradition—of accumulated social knowledge—which the teachings of the world's great religions embody. None of those religions sanctions same-sex marriage.

My friend understood the church-state distinction perfectly well. He was saying, though, that there are traditions and traditions. Male-female marriage is one of the most hallowed. He had no interest in imposing a sectarian religious doctrine on me (as some of the marriage-means-procreation crowd would do); male-female marriage, he was saying, is something much more than a sectarian religious doctrine. Whether you call it a sacrament from God or part of Western civilization's cultural DNA, you are saying essentially the same thing: that, for many people, a same-sex union, whatever else it may be, can never be a marriage, and that no judge or legislature can change this fact.

Here we see peril for same-sex-marriage advocates coming from two directions. On the one side, the Hayekian argument warns of unintended and perhaps grave social consequences if, thinking we're smarter than our customs, we decide to rearrange the core elements of marriage. The current rules for marriage may not be the best ones, and they may even be unfair. But they are all we have, and you cannot reengineer the formula without causing unforeseen results, possibly including the implosion of the institution itself. On the other side, political realism warns that we may do serious damage to the legitimacy of marital law if we rewrite it with disregard for what a large share of Americans recognize as marriage.

Throughout this book I have emphasized the role of social expectations in making marriage work. But people will not expect Frank and Fred to act married if people simply do not take seriously the notion that Frank and Fred are married. Instead, they will see Frank and Fred as a gay couple with a piece of government paper claiming they are married. True, with the marriage license would come the package of legal benefits and entanglements which would help weave the couple's lives together. But that other important element—the element of being married not just in each other's eyes but in society's—would be missing. So same-sex marriage would offer little beyond legal arrangements which could be provided just as well through civil unions, and it might come at a price in diminished respect for the law. If some state passed a law allowing you to marry a Volkswagen, the result would be to make a joke of the law. Certainly legal gay marriage would not seem so silly, but people who found it offensive or illegitimate might just ignore it or, in effect, boycott it. Civil and social marriage would fall out of step. That might not be the end of the world (remember, the vast majority of marriages would be just as they were before), but it could not do marriage or the law any good, either.

Call those, then, the problem of unintended consequences and the problem of legitimacy. They are the toughest problems same-sex marriage has to contend with. But they are not intractable.

––––––––

The Hayekian position really comes in two quite different versions, one much more sweeping than the other. In its strong version, the Hayekian argument implies that no reforms of long-standing insti-tutions or customs should ever be undertaken, because any legal or political meddling would interfere with the natural evolution of social mores. One would thus have had to say, a century and a half ago, that slavery should not be forcibly abolished, because it was customary in almost all human societies. More recently, one would have had to say that the federal government was wrong to step in and end racial segregation instead of letting it evolve at its own pace.

Obviously, neither Hayek nor any reputable follower of his would defend every cultural practice simply on the grounds that it must exist for a reason. Hayekians would point out that slavery violated a fundamental tenet of justice and was intolerably cruel. In calling for slavery's abolition, they do what must be done if they are to be human: they establish a moral standpoint from which to judge social rules and reforms. They thus acknowledge that sometimes society must make changes in the name of fair-ness or decency, even if there are bound to be hidden costs.

If the ban on same-sex marriage were only mildly unfair or if the costs of lifting it were certain to be catastrophic, then the ban could stand on Hayekian grounds. However, if there is any social policy today which has a claim to being scaldingly inhumane, it is the ban on gay marriage. Marriage, after all, is the most funda-mental institution of society and, for most people, an indispensable element of the pursuit of happiness. For the same reason that tinkering with marriage should not be undertaken lightly (marriage is important to personal and social well-being), barring a whole class of people from marrying imposes an extraordinary deprivation. Not so long ago, it was illegal in certain parts of the United States for blacks to marry whites; no one would call this a trivial disenfranchisement. For many years, the champions of women's suffrage were patted on the head and told, "Your rallies and petitions are all very charming, but you don't really *need* to vote, do you?" It didn't wash. The strong Hayekian argument has traction only against a weak moral claim.

To rule out a moral and emotional claim as powerful as the right to marry for love, saying that bad things might happen is not enough. Bad things might always happen. People predicted that bad things would happen if contraception became legal and widespread, and indeed bad things did happen, but that did not make legalizing contraception the wrong thing to do, and, in any case, good things happened also. Unintended consequences can also be positive, after all. The point of this book is that the legalization of same-sex marriage is likely to have many good effects, especially as compared with the alternatives. I may be wrong, but it is not fair to assume only the worst about gay marriage and only the best about a future without it.

Besides, by now the traditional understanding of marriage, however you define it, has been tampered with in all kinds of ways, some of them arguably more consequential than gay marriage is likely to be. No-fault divorce dealt a severe blow to "till death do us part," which was certainly an essential element of the traditional meaning of marriage. It is hard to think of a bigger affront to tradition than allowing married women to own property independently of their husbands. In *What Is Marriage For?*, E. J. Graff quotes a nineteenth-century New York legislator as saying that allowing wives to own property would affront both God and nature, "degrading the holy bonds of matrimony [and] striking at the root of those divinely ordained principles upon which is built the superstructure of our society." In 1844 a New York legislative committee said that permitting married women to control their own property would lead to "infidelity in the marriage bed, a high rate of divorce, and increased female criminality," and would turn marriage "from its high and holy purpose" into something arranged for "convenience and sensuality." A British parliamentarian denounced the proposal as "contrary not only to the law of England but to the law of God." Graff assembles other quotations in the same vein, and goes on to add, wryly, "The funny thing, of course, is that those jeremiads were right." Allowing married women to control their economic destinies did indeed open the door to today's high divorce rates; but it also transformed marriage into something less like servitude for women and more in keeping with liberal principles of equality in personhood and citizenship.

Just an off-the-cuff list of fundamental changes to marriage would include not only divorce and property reform but also the abolition of polygamy, the fading of dowries, the abolition of childhood betrothals, the elimination of parents' right to choose mates for their children or to veto their children's choices, the legalization of interracial marriage, the legalization of contraception, the criminalization of marital rape (an offense that wasn't even recognized until recently), and of course the very concept of civil marriage. Surely it is unfair to say that marriage may be reformed for the sake of anyone and everyone except homosexuals, who must respect the dictates of tradition.

Some people will argue that permitting same-sex marriage would be a more fundamental change than any of the earlier ones. Perhaps so; but equally possible is that we forget today just how unnatural and destabilizing and contrary to the meaning of marriage it once seemed, for example, to put the wife on a par, legally, with the husband. Anyway, even if it is true that gay marriage constitutes a more radical definitional change than earlier innovations, in an important respect it stands out as one of the narrowest of reforms: all the earlier changes directly affected many or all married couples, whereas same-sex marriage would directly pertain to only a small minority. It isn't certain that allowing same-sex couples to marry would have any noticeable effect on heterosexual marriage at all.

True, you never know what might happen when you tinker with tradition. A catastrophe cannot be ruled out. It is worth bearing in mind, though, that predictions of disaster if open homosexuals are integrated into traditionally straight institutions have a perfect track record: they are always wrong. When openly gay couples began making homes together in suburban neighborhoods, the result was not Sodom on every street corner; when they began turning up in corporate jobs, stud collars did not replace neckties. I vividly remember, when I lived in London in 1995, the forecasts of morale and unit cohesion crumbling if open homosexuals were allowed to serve in the British armed forces; but when integration came (under court order), the whole thing turned out to be a nonevent. Again and again, the homosexual threat turns out to be imaginary; straights have far less to fear from gay inclusion than gays do from exclusion. Granted, for many people marriage is defined in terms of sexual orientation, which (for example) employment never was. Still, there is reason to doubt that the latest predictions of the end of civilization will prove more accurate than their predecessors.

So the extreme Hayekian position—never reform anything—is untenable. And that point was made resoundingly by no less an authority than F. A. Hayek himself. In a 1960 essay called "Why I Am Not a Conservative," he took pains to argue that his position was as far from that of reactionary traditionalists as from that of utopian rationalists. "Though there is a need for a 'brake on the vehicle of progress,'" he said, "I personally cannot be content with simply helping to apply the brake." Liberalism (by which he meant classical liberalism, or what many Americans call libertarianism) "has never been a backward-looking doctrine." To the contrary, it recognizes, as reactionary conservatism often fails to, that change is a constant and the world cannot be stopped in its tracks. His own liberalism, he said, "shares with conservatism a distrust of reason to the extent that the liberal is very much aware that we do not know all the answers," but the liberal, unlike the reactionary conservative, does not imagine that simply clinging to the past or "claiming the authority of supernatural sources of knowledge" is any kind of answer. We must move ahead, but humbly and with respect for our own fallibility.

And there are times, he said (in *Law, Legislation, and Liberty*), when what he called "grown law" requires correction by legislation:

> It may be due simply to the recognition that some past development was based on error or that it produced consequences later recognized as unjust. But the most frequent cause is probably that the development of the law has lain in the hands of members of a particular class whose traditional views made them regard as just what could not meet the more general requirements of justice. . . . [S]uch occasions when it is recognized that some hereto accepted rules are unjust in the light of more general principles of justice may well require the revision not only of single rules but of whole sections of the established system of case law.

That passage, I think, could have been written with gay marriage in mind. The old view that homosexuals were heterosexuals who needed punishment or prayer or treatment has been exposed as an error. What homosexuals need is the love of another homosexual. The ban on same-sex marriage, hallowed though it is, no longer accords with liberal justice or the meaning of marriage as it is practiced today. Something has to give. Standing still is not an option.

Hayek himself, then, was a partisan of the milder version of Hayekianism. This version is not so much a prescription as an attitude. Respect tradition. Reject utopianism. Plan for mistakes rather than for perfection. If reform is needed, look for paths that follow the terrain of custom, if possible. If someone promises to remake society on rational or supernatural or theological principles, run in the opposite direction. In sum: move ahead, but be careful.

Good advice. But not advice, particularly, against gay marriage. Remember Hayek's admonition against dogmatic conservatism. In a shifting current, holding your course can be just as dangerous as oversteering. As I have often said in this book, conservatives, in their panic to stop same-sex marriage, jeopardize marriage's universality and ultimately its legitimacy. They are taking risks, and big ones, and unnecessary ones. The liberal tradition and the Declaration of Independence are not currents which you want to set marriage against.

It is worth recalling that Burke, the patron saint of social conservatism and the scourge of the French Revolution, supported the American Revolution. He distinguished between a revolt which aimed to overthrow established rights and principles and a revolt which aimed to restore them. Many of the American founders, incidentally, made exactly the same distinction. Whatever else they may have been, they were not utopian social engineers. Whether a modern-day Burke or Jefferson would support gay marriage, I cannot begin to say; but I am confident they would, at least, have understood and carefully weighed the possibility that to preserve the liberal foundation of civil marriage, we may find it necessary to adjust its boundaries.

———

The problem of legitimacy remains. What happens if you adjust the boundaries of civil marriage but social marriage (including religious marriage) fails to follow? The answer, I think, belongs in the next chapter, because the trick is in the transition.

_____

10

Getting It Right

S orting through the pros and cons, here is where I think we wind up:

1. Gay marriage may bring both harms and benefits. Because it has never been tried in the United States, Americans have no way to know just what would happen. Everybody can make guesses and arguments, but real life has a way of tripping up even the cleverest prognosticators. As F. A. Hayek warns, the problem must be approached with a healthy respect for what we do not know, and an even healthier respect for what we think we know but don't.

2. In the past, predictions of catastrophe following the integration of openly gay people into mainstream social institutions have been consistently wrong. The sky never falls. Moreover, most of the arguments asserting that gay marriage would harm straight marriage seem overblown, at best, often just fanciful, and sometimes hypocritical, as evinced by the fact that heterosexuals rarely apply to themselves the marital qualifications which gay marriage opponents insist on applying to homosexuals. But you never know. It is always possible that gay marriage

could be calamitous, and with an institution as important as marriage, you can't count on getting a second chance.

3. On the other hand, perpetuating the ban on same-sex marriage may have baleful consequences of its own. It might substantially weaken the special status on which marriage depends, at a time when marriage is facing more than enough competition. The ban has already given a boost to the alternatives-to-marriage movement and will continue to do so. Also, it links marriage with discrimination at a time when, throughout the liberal world, discrimination is sinking into disrepute. Continuing the prohibition, moreover, would force homosexuals to bear a painful burden of exclusion from the benefits which marriage uniquely brings—benefits which would accrue to society as well.

4. Just doing nothing—"leaving marriage alone"—does not avoid the problem, because calling a halt to social and cultural change is not an option. When you are at sea in a fog, closing your eyes does not help.

Investors face this kind of situation all the time. They recognize they must put their money somewhere, and so they look for strategies which minimize the chance of catastrophic loss without foreclosing the possibility of unexpected gain. If someone said, "Investing is risky, so I keep all my money under the mattress," they would be quick to explain that the mattress strategy is risky, too, and costly in terms of opportunities forgone.

Perhaps the most striking oddity of the gay-marriage debate, when you think about it, is that most people consider only *whether* and never *how*. They treat same-sex marriage as a yes-no, on-off proposition. You can be fairly sure a public-policy debate is in its infancy when people talk about only two options—namely, all or nothing. Gay people, of course, want full legal equality, which would mean having the unquestioned right to same-sex marriage throughout the United States. The opponents of same-sex marriage insist that even a single gay marriage anywhere on American soil would effectively impose gay marriage everywhere. Because they have adopted a scorched-earth, stop-it-at-all-costs mind-set, they regard even discussing the question of *how* as a surrender. That is what happens when you panic: you miss opportunities to make the most of your situation and turn change to your benefit.

As any investor, gambler, or military commander will tell you, decisions made in a panic are almost invariably poor decisions. The all-or-nothing debate on same-sex marriage ignores an important question: Could same-sex marriage be managed in a way which maximizes the benefits and minimizes the risks? As it happens, the answer to that question is yes. Not only is there such a strategy, but the United States is uniquely suited to adopt it. Let the states try same-sex marriage individually, if and when they are inclined to do so. The decentralized approach is not only in keeping with the country's most venerable legal traditions; it also improves the odds of getting gay marriage right, in three ways: experimental, social, and political.

———

First, the *experimental*. Nothing terrible—in fact, nothing even noticeable—seems to have happened to marriage since Vermont began allowing gay civil unions. But civil unions are not marriage. The only way to learn what happens when same-sex couples take out a marriage license is to let some of them do it. Turning marriage into a giant national experiment seems rash, but trying it in a few states gives them and the rest of the country a chance to watch and learn. Will the divorce rate rise or the marriage rate fall? Before long, we should get some indications. Moreover, states offer the resources of variety: they are, as the saying goes, the laboratories of democracy. One state might go with flat legalization. Another might make some special provisions (for instance, regarding child custody or adoption). A third might offer counseling or other assistance (not out of line with a growing movement to offer social-service support to so-called fragile families). Variety would thus provide much useful information. Where does gay marriage work best? What kind of community support does it need? What are the avoidable pitfalls? Just as states led the way with welfare reform—their mistakes teaching us as much as their successes—so they should lead the way with marriage reform.

Either to forbid same-sex marriage nationwide or to mandate it nationwide would be to throw away a wealth of information about marriage, gay and straight. Hayek would likely not have approved. He urged allowing social change to evolve from below, rather than either blocking it or imposing it from above. In America, the states are where such evolution happens.

No less important is the *social* benefit of letting the states find their own way. Here, I believe, is the answer to the problem of legitimacy. Law is only part of what gives marriage its binding power; community support and social expectations are as significant. In a community which looked on same-sex marriage with bafflement or outright hostility, a gay couple's marriage license would help solve some of their legal problems but would leave the social supports missing. The couple and the community would both be shortchanged.

The answer is to let gay marriage take root at its own pace, in communities which are ready to accept same-sex couples into the fellowship of matrimony. As anyone knows who has looked recently at a blue-versus-red national electoral map, states, for all their internal heterogeneity, retain quite different social and cultural characters. Utah is not at all like Vermont. Letting states choose gay marriage does not guarantee that everyone in the state will recognize the marriage as legitimate, but it pretty well ensures that gay married couples will find communities which embrace their unions and that a large share of people in the state will look upon same-sex marriage as legitimate. It thus maximizes the odds that the marriages will take root in receptive soil.

Third, the *political* benefit of a state-by-state approach is not to be underestimated. This is the benefit of avoiding a national culture war.

The United States is not (thank goodness) a culturally homogeneous country. It consists of many distinct moral communities. On touchy social issues, such as abortion and homosexuality, people don't agree and probably never will, and the signal political advantage of the federalist system is that it does not require them to agree. They can agree to disagree. Individuals and groups who find the values or laws of one state obnoxious have the sovereign right to live somewhere else. For many years, until real-estate prices finally got the better of my principles, I refused to live in Virginia because of the offense I took at Virginia's sodomy law. Partly to be in a place whose law I found morally congenial, I lived in the District of Columbia and paid higher taxes.

The nationalization of abortion policy in the Supreme Court's 1973 *Roe v. Wade* decision remains a textbook example of the bitter and abiding culture war that can be set off when conscientious objectors are given nowhere to go. If the Supreme Court had not stepped in, abortion would today be legal in most states, but in a few states prolifers would have the comfort of knowing that they, too, could find a home—not everywhere, but somewhere. Instead of an unending cultural schism infecting every Supreme Court nomination and most political jurisdictions, we would see occasional local flare-ups in state legislatures or courtrooms.

America is a stronger country for the moral diversity that federalism uniquely allows. Moral law and family law govern the most intimate and, often, controversial spheres of life. For the sake of domestic tranquillity, domestic law is best left to the level of government that is closest to home.

———

So well suited is the federalist system to the gay-marriage issue that it might almost have been set up to handle it. And, in a round-about way, it was.

The Founders, of course, had no inkling of gay marriage, or for that matter of what we call gayness, but they knew all about controversial and intractable social issues. Their biggest headache was in coping with a moral issue on which feelings ran high and no national consensus was possible: slavery. Slavery was not remotely like same-sex marriage substantively, but it did pose the same sorts of political problems. What do you do when you cannot expect moral agreement, when each side's notion of justice is anathema to the other, when change might be disruptive, but when standing still is not an option? In an uneasy compromise, the Founders left the issue of slavery to the states. It was, in hindsight, a stain on the Constitution, but at the time it looked like the best hope of avoiding a national schism. In time, the Founders hoped, evolving consensus and economic modernization might dissolve slavery in the states which clung to it.

The strategy failed. It was done in by the controversy over slavery in newly admitted states, by the rise of the great cotton plantations in the South, and by the sheer moral intractability of the "peculiar institution" itself. Nearly a century after the Civil War, in the civil rights movement, the federal government had to step in when white southerners met peaceful black protests with violence and vindictiveness. Then came the abortion dispute, another vexing moral issue on which consensus was impossible. In that case, the federalist approach was well on its way to working when the Supreme Court, in *Roe v. Wade,* kicked success away, a mistake for which the country and the Court are still paying.

And here at last, with same-sex marriage, is an opportunity to get it right—combined with another campaign to kick success away.

In the United States, marriage has been the exclusive domain of state law not just since the days of the founders but since colonial times, before the states were states. In a new land whose Puritans and Presbyterians and Anglicans and deists answered to different religious callings, it would have made no sense to centralize marriage or family law. To my knowledge, only twice has the federal government overruled the states on marriage. The first time was when it required Utah to ban polygamy as a condition for joining the union, an exception which proves the rule, because the imperative was to make the change *before* Utah became a state. The second time was with the Supreme Court's 1967 decision, in *Loving v. Virginia,* striking down sixteen states' bans on interracial marriage. Here the Court said not that marriage should be defined by the federal government but only that states were not free to define marriage in a way which violated core constitutional rights. It was as if a state had tried to say that people can marry only if they give up the right to vote or to criticize the government. On the one occasion when Congress directly addressed same-sex marriage, in the Defense of Marriage Act (1996), it decreed that the federal government would not recognize same-sex marriages but took care not to impose the same rule on the states.

Today, marriage laws (and, of course, divorce laws) continue to be set by the states and differ on many points, from age of consent to who may marry whom. In Arizona, for example, first cousins are allowed to marry only if both are older than sixty-five or if the couple can prove to a judge "that one of the cousins is unable to reproduce." (So much for marriage's being about procreation. Here is a state invoking sterility as a condition for marriage!) Conventional wisdom notwithstanding, the Constitution does not require states to recognize each other's marriages. The Full Faith and Credit clause (Article IV, Section 1) requires states to recognize each other's public acts and judgments. "However," notes Dale Carpenter, a constitutional law professor at the University of Minnesota, "the Full Faith and Credit clause has never been interpreted to mean that every state must recognize every marriage performed in every other state. Every state reserves the right to refuse to recognize a marriage performed in another state if that marriage would violate the state's public policy."

This public-policy exception, as it is called, is only common sense. If each state could legislate for all the rest, American-style federalism would be at an end. Under federalism, if Delaware (for example) decided to lower its minimum age for marriage to ten, no other state would need to regard a ten-year-old as legally married. Ditto if Idaho legalized plural marriages. In 1939 and again in 1988 (according to the conservative legal analyst Bruce Fein), the Supreme Court ruled that the Full Faith and Credit clause does not compel a state "to substitute the statutes of other states for its own statutes dealing with a subject matter concerning which it is competent to legislate." A lawyer who researched the matter told me, "I have not found a single case where a federal court has forced another state to recognize a marriage where the state asserts that said marriage would violate the public policy of the state."

If all that were not enough, the Full Faith and Credit clause itself specifically gives Congress an oversight role in determining when states must recognize each other's laws and judgments. The Constitution's wording is somewhat opaque: "The Congress may by general laws prescribe the manner in which such [state] acts, records, and proceedings shall be proved, and the effect thereof." The courts have not yet determined what exactly this statement means, but plainly it gives Congress a voice, and so the courts must consider the fact that Congress has spoken: in 1996, in the Defense of Marriage Act, Congress specifically decreed that no state would have to recognize any other state's same-sex marriage.

Why, then, do the states all recognize each other's marriages? Not because they must but because they choose to. Before the gay-marriage controversy arose, the country was favored with a consensus on the terms of marriage. Interstate differences were small enough so that states saw no need to split hairs, and mutual recognition was certainly a major convenience. (In fact, states arguably got lazy in waving through each other's divorce reforms.) Gay marriage, of course, changes the picture, by asking states to reconsider a fundamental boundary of legal marriage. This is just the sort of controversy in which the Framers imagined states could and often should go their separate ways; and going their different ways is what will happen under the law as it is and as it long has been.

As so often seems to be the case, the gay left and the antigay right, nominally bitter adversaries, have a way of working together against the center. They may agree on little else, but, where marriage is concerned, they both want the federal government to take over.

To some gay people, the idea of anything less than nationwide recognition of same-sex marriage seems both impractical and unjust. "Wait a minute," they say. "How is this supposed to work? I get married in Maryland (say), but every time I cross the border into Virginia on my morning commute, I'm suddenly single? Am I married, then, or not? What a mess! Portability is one of the distinctive attributes that make marriage different from, say, civil unions. If it's not portable, it isn't really marriage at all. It's second-class citizenship. Obviously, as soon as same-sex marriage is approved in any one state, we're going to sue in federal court to have it recognized in all the others. Why should we expect any less than the prerogatives straight couples take for granted?"

"Just so!" reply some conservatives. "Gay activists have no intention of settling for marriage in just one or two states. They want the whole ball of wax—and why wouldn't they? They will just keep suing until they find some activist federal judge (and there are plenty) who agrees with them. Public-policy exception and Defense of Marriage Act or no, the courts, not least the Supreme Court, do as they please, and lately they have signed on to the gay cultural agenda. Besides, deciding state by state is impractical; the gay activists are right about that. Even if the federal courts managed to stay out, the sheer inconvenience of dealing with couples who go in and out of matrimony every time they cross state lines will drive states to the lowest common denominator, and gay marriages will wind up being recognized everywhere. In this situation, federalism is impossible. The only choice is between nationwide gay marriage, possibly imposed by the courts, and a constitutional amendment banning same-sex marriage throughout the country."

Whoa. As my four-year-old niece likes to say, "Calm down, everybody." Whenever you hear activists at two extremes insisting there is no middle ground, go lock up the family silver. Chances are you're being hustled.

Neither of the two arguments I have just sketched is without merit. But both sides are asking the country to presume in advance that the Founders were wrong and to foreclose the possibility that seems most likely to succeed. It is as if someone had said, in 1789, "Who are you kidding? There's no middle ground on slavery, so let's just split into two countries right now, or else go ahead and have a civil war and get it over with." It turned out to be true that slavery admitted of no middle ground, but if the Founders had started out from that presumption, the United States as we know it would never have been born. Or what if someone said, in the late 1960s, "You can't have the states doing fifty different things about abortion; it's impractical and unfair. So let's just have the federal government write a single policy into the Constitution." Which is exactly what happened, via *Roe v. Wade* and other Supreme Court decisions. That didn't work out so well, either.

The simple answer—really not simple at all—to both schools of all-or-nothing activists is just this: try federalism first. If state-by-state incrementalism fails, there will always be time for national solutions later on. Neither side can be blamed for wanting to impose its moral vision on the whole country and for hoping to preempt any mixed or moderate alternative, but the nation would be unwise to let either side have its way. Memo to federal judges (especially those on the Supreme Court): do us all a favor, and butt out. Memo to constitutional amenders: do us all a favor, and butt out.

The problem is that both sides want something which life doesn't usually offer—a guarantee. Gay-marriage supporters want a guarantee of full legal equality, and gay-marriage opponents want a guarantee that same-sex marriage will never happen. I can't offer any guarantees. But I can offer some reassurance.

Is a state-by-state approach impractical and unsustainable? Possibly, but the right time to deal with problems would be when (or if) they arise. Going in, however, there is little reason to foresee any great difficulty. There are many precedents for state-by-state action. The country currently operates under a tangle of different state banking laws. As any banker will tell you, the lack of uniformity has made national banking more difficult. But as you may have noticed, we do have banks. Long ago, bankers got used to meeting different requirements in different states. To take another example: California, alone among the states, passed a law not long ago requiring automobile manufacturers to sell zero-emission vehicles. Car companies groused, but no one said, "That's impossible! You can't let different states set different pollution rules. It would be much too inconvenient." Contract law, property law, and criminal law all vary significantly among the states. Variety is the point of federalism. Uniform national policies may look convenient, but they risk sticking us with the same wrong approach everywhere.

My guess is that, if one or two states allowed gay marriage, there would be a confusing transitional period while state courts and legislatures worked out what to do, quickly followed, in all but a few places, by the establishment of routines which everyone would soon take for granted. If New Jersey adopted gay marriage, for instance, New York would have a number of options. It might ban recognition of gay marriage, as thirty-seven states have, in fact, preemptively done. It might recognize New Jersey's same-sex marriages. Or it might honor certain aspects of New Jersey's gay marriage—say, medical power of attorney and inheritance and tenancy rights—while disallowing others. A state which had a civil-union or domestic-partner program, as Vermont does, might automatically subsume under that program any gay couple who had married in New Jersey. My fairly confident expectation is that initially most states would reject out-of-state gay marriages (as indeed they have done, in advance of any actual enactment), but a handful might accept them, and a larger handful might choose an intermediate option.

For married gay couples, variation in state acceptance would be a real nuisance. If I got married to a man in Maryland but worked in Virginia, I would need to be aware of the difference in marriage laws and make arrangements—medical power of attorney, a will, and whatnot—for when I was out of state. Pesky and, yes, unfair (or at least unequal). And, outside my home state, the clear line between being married and not being married would to some extent have been blurred. In Virginia, people who saw my wedding band would not be sure if I was "really married" or just "Maryland married." The situation would not be ideal, especially if you believe, as I do, that marriage works best as a bright-line designation.

Even so, gay marriage would be far from impotent. Even in Virginia, people who saw my ring and learned I was "Maryland married" would know I had made the Big Commitment in my home state, and thus in the eyes of my community and its law. They would know I had gone beyond cohabitation or even domestic partnership and that I was governed by the same divorce laws as any other married couple in my state. As a Jew, I may not recognize the spiritual authority of a Catholic priest, but I do recognize the special commitment he has made to his faith and his community, and I respect him for that. In much the same way, even out-of-state gay marriages would command an additional increment of respect.

When you are starving, one or two slices of bread may not be as good as fifty, but they are a different proposition from having no bread at all. The damage which the alienation from marriage has done to gay culture and gay lives comes not just from knowing we can't marry right now and right here but from knowing we can't ever hope to marry at all. When the first state adopts full-fledged same-sex marriage, gay life will have changed forever.

Marriage will have gone from impossible to possible. The full benefits of same-sex marriage will come only when it is legal everywhere: that is how to make marriage not just possible for gay people but expected. Yet the benefits are not all-or-nothing. They begin with the first state's announcement that, in *this* community, marriage is for everyone.

Of course, I would love nothing better than to have people across America read this book, come to their senses, and say, "Rauch is right, let's have gay marriage everywhere now." I would like to see laws passed by acclamation in all fifty states next week. Back on planet Earth, however, I know that building consensus takes time. Nationwide imposition of same-sex marriage by a federal court might discredit both gay marriage and the courts, as well as starting a long-lasting culture war like the one over abortion—only, perhaps, bigger. My confidence in the public's decency and in its unfailing, if sometimes slow-acting, commitment to liberal principles is robust. To me, the pace states set will be too slow. It will be far from ideal. Yet it will be something much more important than ideal: it will be right.

Is it inevitable that federal courts will order same-sex marriage? That is what many conservatives fear, which is why they say they want a constitutional amendment to head off the courts.

These days we should accept as facts of life that someone will sue over anything, that some court will hear any lawsuit, and that there is just no telling what a court might do. For all we know, some court might order people to wear their underwear on the outside. Like many Americans since the 1980s, I have switched from worrying about excessive judicial passivity to worrying about excessive judicial activism. Despite my enthusiasm for same-sex marriage, I would hate to see the Supreme Court impose it on an unwilling nation.

But we typically reserve constitutional amendments for the most likely or imminent threats to liberty, justice, or popular sovereignty. That the Supreme Court might impose same-sex marriage on an unwilling nation may not be quite as unlikely as its imposing an underwear-on-the-outside requirement, but it is right up there. All precedent, going back to colonial times, leaves marriage to the states. All precedent supports the public-policy exception. The Constitution specifically gives Congress oversight, and Congress has affirmed the public-policy exception. A court which wanted to mandate interstate recognition of gay marriages would need to burn through three separate firewalls. Even for an activist court, that is tough. The current Supreme Court, moreover, has proved particularly fierce in resisting federal incursions into states' authority.

That, as I said, is no guarantee of future judicial restraint; but no federal court has ever ruled in favor of gay marriage, and to my knowledge none has claimed the authority to mandate it or shown any inclination to do so. If we are going to get into the business of constitutionally banning anything that someone imagines the Supreme Court might one day mandate, we will need a Constitution the size of a phone book.

If the federal courts did seem likely to mandate same-sex marriage nationwide, wouldn't a constitutional ban be the answer? Certainly not. If the problem is to keep federal courts out of the gay-marriage business, doing so would be easy enough. All you need is an amendment saying: "Nothing in this Constitution requires the federal government or any state to recognize anything other than the union of one man and one woman as a marriage." End of problem, if there was one. The states and Washington could all go their separate ways. Actually, such an amendment would merely emphasize what is already the law of the land, but if conservatives are worried about lawless courts, that amendment ought to settle the issue.

Instead, some conservatives lined up behind a proposed amendment whose operative sentence read: "Marriage in the United States shall consist only of the union of a man and a woman." As is immediately apparent, this was the very opposite of a states' rights amendment. It would ban states from trying gay marriage even if every politician and voter in the state wanted it. On any number of counts, the constitutional ban was a radical idea. It would usurp three centuries of state sovereignty over marriage law. It would write social policy into the Constitution. It would guarantee a future of proliferating competitors to marriage. It would ignite a national culture war. It would foreclose all options short of all-or-nothing.

Social conservatives have lost one cultural battle after another in the past five decades: divorce, abortion, pornography, gambling, school prayer, homosexuality. They have seen how strings and snares come with every federal takeover of state and local prerogatives. They have learned all too well the power of centralization to quash moral diversity. And here they were, saying they would risk the likely consequences of Uncle Sam's intervention in civil matrimony rather than let a single gay couple marry on any square inch of American territory. Why would they do this?

Not, I suspect, because they fear gay marriage would fail. Rather, because they fear it would succeed.

———

In debating same-sex marriage, conservative opponents sometimes raise an objection which I think is revealing. "Even if federal courts don't mandate gay marriage," they say, "it will still spread. States will just find it too inconvenient to maintain different standards." I already mentioned why I think inconvenience is unlikely to force the issue one way or another. But here let me make a deeper point.

States recognized each other's divorce reforms in the 1960s and 1970s without giving the matter a whole lot of thought (which was too bad). The likelihood they would recognize another state's same-sex marriages without a serious debate, by contrast, approximates zero, especially at first. Later, as time goes on, states might get used to gay marriage. They might indeed begin to wave it through as a convenience for all concerned. If that happened, however, it could only be because gay marriage turned out not to be the end of the world. It might even be because gay marriage seemed to be working pretty well. "That isn't so bad," Virginia might say, five or ten or twenty years after Maryland began allowing gay marriages. "We're not ready to perform legal same-sex marriages here. But we can recognize Maryland's." This would not be contagion. It would be adoption. Flexibility is the point of federalism. Try something here or there. If it works, let it spread. If it fails, let it fade.

In other words, the very reason I support the federalist approach is the reason anti-gay-marriage hard-liners oppose it. They want to stop the experiment from ever beginning. Repeat: ever. If you care about finding the best way forward for marriage and for gay people in a changing world, that posture is hard to justify.

One rationale, I suppose, might be: "Gay marriage is so certain to be a calamity that even the smallest trial anywhere should be banned." To me, that smacks more of hysteria than of rational thought. If there is any good evidence to support the idea that allowing some gay marriages somewhere must bring the collapse of marriage everywhere, the Chicken Little crowd has yet to produce it. When extreme environmentalists demand a preemptive and total ban on all bioengineered foods forever, conservatives cluck at their irrationalism and fear mongering, and quite rightly. In the 1980s and early 1990s, some liberals were sure that reforming the welfare system would put millions of children out on the street. In the face of inevitable calamity, even trying welfare reform, they said, was irresponsible. Fortunately, the states didn't listen. They experimented—responsibly.

The stronger objection cites not certain catastrophe but insidious decay. "Ah," a conservative once said to me, "changes in complicated institutions like marriage, as you yourself point out, take years to work their way through society. They are often subtle. Social scientists will argue until the cows come home about the positive and negative effects of gay marriage. So states might adopt or recognize it before they fully understood the harm it does."

Actually, you can usually tell pretty fast what a major policy change is doing—at least, you can get a general idea. States knew quite quickly that welfare reforms were working better than the old program. That was why the idea caught on. If same-sex marriage really is going to cause problems, some of them should be visible to the naked eye within a few years of the reform.

Even setting that point aside, however, notice how the terms of the discussion have shifted. Now the problem is not that gay marriage will cause sudden, catastrophic harm but that it will cause subtle, slow damage. In fact, the damage may be barely discernible. Well, there may be subtle and slow benefits, too. But there will certainly be one large and quick benefit: *the benefit to gay people of being able to get married.* To overlook that large and quick benefit is like saying, "Letting women vote may or may not have improved turnout rates and electoral outcomes, and we're not really sure, so there's no telling whether women's suffrage was a worthwhile idea." If what we are doing is excluding a whole segment of the population from arguably the most important of all civic institutions, we would have to do so because the group's participation would cause severe disruptions—certainly, in any case, noticeable ones. If, on the other hand, the burden is on gay people to prove that same-sex marriage never causes even minor difficulty, regardless of the great good it may do for homosexuals, then we are back to single-entry bookkeeping, where *any* cost to heterosexuals, however small, outweighs *every* benefit to homosexuals, however large. That gay people's welfare counts should, of course, be obvious, but sometimes people do seem to need to be reminded.

I fully expect same-sex marriage to have many subtle ramifications, good, bad, and indifferent. I do not expect social science to sort them all out. But the fact that the world is complicated is the very reason to run the experiment, not to ban it. You might as well say, "Welfare reform will have many subtle effects, so we'd better not try it." Indeed, we never know for sure what the effects of any public policy will be, and so we do a limited experiment if possible and decide on the basis of necessarily imperfect information.

And—an important point—*who* decides? Conservative intellectuals? Left-wing activists? Washington bureaucrats? University experts? You? Me? None of the above. Where marriage is concerned, the sovereign right to deem a policy successful or failed belongs to the people of the states. It is for them to judge whether same-sex marriage is an experiment worth trying, whether it has worked in their state, and whether it deserves adoption or recognition.

I am happy to place the future of gay marriage in the hands of the people of the several states, because I am confident of two things. First, within my lifetime, and probably fairly soon, at least one state will adopt same-sex marriage the old-fashioned and best way, by passing a bill in the legislature. That will signal substantial social support. (If a state judge, acting under a state constitution, imposed same-sex marriage in the face of widespread public opposition, that would be the state's business—after all, states can change their constitutions and replace judges—but it would not be good policy, and it might leave gay marriage without enough community support to work well.) Second, when a state embraces same-sex marriage, the sky will not fall. Civilization will not tumble into the sea. The divorce and illegitimacy rates will not double. They will not even change noticeably. Other states will notice this. They will see married gay couples woven into the fabric of their communities. They will see the rise of a gay-responsibility culture and the decline of the same-sex underworld. They will hear from parents who want the benefits of marriage for their gay children. Slowly at first, and then with enthusiasm, more states will embrace gay marriage—not because they have to, but because it works.

If conservatives oppose same-sex marriage on grounds of prudence, then the response must be to try it where people are comfortable with it and believe they can make it work. To insist that gays will wreck traditional marriage without ever letting them prove otherwise is like denying someone a driver's license because you insist he is blind, and then refusing him a vision test. If, on the other hand, conservatives oppose same-sex marriage because it is immoral and would be wrong by definition, no matter what its real-world impact, fine, but let them say so. Let them have the honesty to acknowledge that they are not fighting for the good of marriage so much as using marriage as a weapon in their fight against homosexuals.

———

A few words, finally, about "marriage-lite." You may have noticed a tension between two of my positions. On the one hand, I argue that gay marriage is important partly because it will short-circuit the movement to create alternatives to marriage. On the other hand, I argue for a state-by-state approach, which would take a long time, leaving plenty of opportunity for quasi-marriages to establish themselves (as seems to be the trend) and tempting states to set up alternatives as a way to fend off gay marriage (as happened in Vermont). If same-sex marriage takes several decades to get established, might it not come along too late to have much effect on marriage-lite?

It might. All I can say is that we live in an imperfect world. The more quickly people can be persuaded to open legal marriage to homosexuals, the less legitimacy and political pull the alternatives will have. That said, it takes as long as it takes. One thing is clear: the ban on same-sex marriage, for however long it lasts, guarantees a major new market for cohabitation and marriage-lite, and legitimizes their incursion into old markets. Hayek wrote (in "Why I Am Not a Conservative"), "What a liberal must ask, first of all, is not how fast or how far we should move, but where we should move." If we want a future with more marriage rather than less, granting marriage's competitors a monopoly on new markets cannot possibly be the right course.

Gay marriage will let air out of the tires of the alternatives-to-marriage movement, but that by itself is not enough. The sooner the better, states should not only legalize gay marriage but simultaneously withdraw any public-sector alternatives, on the grounds that they are no longer necessary. Private-sector employers should do the same. "Domestic-partner benefits exist only to fill a gap," the politicians and executives should say, "and now that gap is gone." Domestic-partner programs should go down in history as a transition, not a destination.

Politically, can it be done? Clearly, gay marriage is the only hope, and even then it won't be easy. But that, as Hayek might have said, is where we should move. If you want the benefits of marriage, *get married*—no exclusions, no exceptions. Moving from here to there in the next few decades, as fast as the public consensus will allow but no faster: that is how to score the win-win-win.

11

A Golden Anniversary

One way or another, whether approaching from the front, rear, or side, this book again and again finds itself bumping up against different versions of basically the same question:

Can marriage be saved from its friends?

Perhaps I should say, from its putative friends. I don't doubt that the people who insist on "defending" marriage from homosexuals sincerely believe they are defending marriage itself. And yet their claim to be doing marriage a favor is at best questionable. Locking same-sex couples out of marriage will inevitably—almost by definition—give impetus to a host of competitors while adding a discriminatory tarnish to marriage. Try as hard as I might, I have a hard time seeing how this course could be good for marriage as an institution. More likely, it is just the sort of historic wrong turn which opponents of gay marriage say they want to avoid.

I said earlier in the book, and I think it bears repeating: the river of history has rounded a bend. We have a choice to make. Marriage can be universal and thus *the* norm for serious couples, or it can be exclusive and thus only one of several norms for serious couples. But it cannot be both, and there are risks on both sides. We need to stop hyperventilating, sit down, think hard, and get this right.

In the introduction, I mentioned what I called the imagination gap: straight people's difficulty imagining life without marriage, gay people's difficulty imagining life with it. That imagination gap is conjoined with another. To imagine a future with same-sex marriage is difficult, because same-sex marriage is such a new idea (as new as the modern view of homosexuality itself); but to imagine a future without same-sex marriage is not hard at all. And so one future seems radical, the other mundane. Prudent people shrink from the unknown, and thank goodness for that—up to a point. Thinking people, though, have a duty to remember that a future without marriage for gay couples is also a leap into the unknown. It leaps into a future in which a new legal and social infrastructure grows up outside marriage; in which various forms of socially and legally sanctioned nonmarriage become, for all homosexual couples and many heterosexual couples, substitutes for marriage; in which a wedding band might mean married or civilly united or domestically partnered or just "committed"; in which "traditional marriage" becomes only one color on the lifestyle palette; in which polite people no longer ask each other whether they are married but, more discreetly, whether they are "partnered" or "coupled" or "with someone." Imagine that.

One day Aaron, who was six, asked me a question for which I was unprepared. "Why do you and Uncle Michael live together?"

Aaron is Michael's nephew. He and his family visit us every year or so, and most years we all go camping together; I have known him since he was two, so we have become fixtures in each other's lives. He is bright and inquisitive and doesn't miss much. It was one day when I was reading to him from *Through the Looking Glass* and he was instructing me on the characteristics of the planets that he asked why Uncle Michael and I live together. I thought for only half a second before replying, "Because we love each other."

At the time, I was pretty pleased with that answer, and Aaron seemed satisfied with it. Only later, as I collected my thoughts for this book, did I begin to have my doubts. To Aaron, the message must have been: if two people love each other, they live together. Love and cohabitation. They go together like a horse and transportation. Is this such a good message for a child to grow up with? I began to imagine, instead, that I had been able to answer, "Because we're married, silly!" Aaron was old enough so that the idea of two men being married would have needed some explaining. I would have told him, perhaps, "Your Uncle Michael and I love each other and so we got married, just the way your mother and father did and just the way you will someday." Love and marriage. They go together.

Aaron knows who I am, and he knows who his Uncle Michael is, but he does not know who *we* are. We are "living together," but why? To be married is not to need to answer that question, because no one thinks to ask it. I was unprepared for Aaron's query because, without being able to offer the ready-made handle of marriage, explaining a homosexual relationship to a child is difficult. Explaining a heterosexual relationship isn't always much easier. A six-year-old knows that his parents or the couple next door are married, but he does not want or need to know about their relationship. Marriage clarifies the world by allowing people to acknowledge each other's unions without needing to know what goes on inside them, because marriage, uniquely, defines a relation, not a relationship. I thought later: Can it be good for Aaron to grow up in a world where there are so many shapeless relationships which need explaining? To my niece, Caitlyn, who is four, Michael is Uncle Michael. In a few years, without the handle of marriage to give her, how will I or her mother explain why Michael is Uncle Michael?

My imagination, now running, turns to a world in which Aaron and Caitlyn understand from early childhood that their uncles are married. Later on, one of them may fall in love with a boy or a girl instead of a girl or a boy. Nothing will make the discovery of

homosexual longings easy for a young person; but Aaron or Caitlyn, having grown up with married Uncle Jon and Uncle Michael
in their lives, would know something I never did: that a future
awaits them in marriage. The road ahead beckons not into a
wilderness but toward a home and a community.

Probably they are straight. (Most people are.) Probably, in the
fullness of time, they will have children of their own. If Caitlyn
had a gay son, he would grow up with a double benefit: his own
expectation of marrying, and his parents' similar expectation for
him. Caitlyn, grown and a mother, would have friends or colleagues or neighbors who were gay and legally married. She would
want nothing less for her son. She would say to her boy, as mothers have said for generations, not "someday if you get married"
but "someday *when* you get married." Uncle Jon and Uncle
Michael, if they were still around, would attend the young man's
wedding and have a good cry.

———

The first generation to be fully at home with same-sex marriage
will not be today's adults or even today's children but the new-
borns who open their eyes in a world where gay couples can wed.
Not all of them will grow up believing that homosexuality is moral
or that it is as good as heterosexuality, but most of them will come
to believe that marriage is better than nonmarriage, for heterosexuals and homosexuals alike. Recognizing as much, many houses of
worship will bless gay unions and welcome them into the community's fellowship. The full social benefits of gay marriage will come
when religions as well as governments customarily bless it: when
women marry women in big church ceremonies as parents weep
and ministers, solemnly smiling, intone the vows. Far from being
abolished or trivialized, the vows will be renewed.

I probably won't live to see it, but someday will come the first
same-sex golden wedding anniversary. Then will come a few more,
first a trickle and then a flood. Not just the couples but their

families and friends and neighbors and colleagues will gather to celebrate the noblest achievement that ordinary people can attain: the successful dedication of two lives to each other. On that fiftieth anniversary, when the golden bells peal, homosexuality will have ceased to exist as a distinct and problematic human condition. There will remain only what matters: the years of comforting, of caring, of worrying, of fighting, of holding one another in the dark, till death do us part. As Golde said to Tevye, and to a small boy who believed he would never marry: if that's not love, what is?

Index

About the Author

JONATHAN RAUCH is a correspondent for *The Atlantic Monthly*, a senior writer and columnist for *National Journal*, and a writer in residence at the Brookings Institution. He is the author of several previous books on public policy, culture, and economics, including, most recently, *Government's End: Why Washington Stopped Working*. His work has appeared in *The New Republic*, *The Economist*, *Harper's*, *Reason*, *Fortune*, *The New York Times*, *The Washington Post*, *The Wall Street Journal*, and *Slate*, among other publications. He is vice president of the Independent Gay Forum and lives outside Washington, D.C.